CW00500591

Mike Oakley was born and brought up in Weymouth before moving to Bristol in the mid 1960s, where he worked in town and country planning until retiring in 1996. In recent years he has developed a keen interest in the history and role of railway stations and halts, particularly in his home county of Dorset and in the area around Bristol and Bath. As a result, he has built up a substantial library of photographs of Dorset's stations, a small selection of which are reproduced in this book. He is also the author of *Bristol Suburban* (1990), an illustrated account of the city's stations and halts.

Following page
Blandford Forum Station, August 1960.
The train is Class 9F 2-10-0 No 92204, the 'up' 'Pines Express'.

DISCOVER DORSET

RAILWAY STATIONS

MIKE OAKLEY

THE DOVECOTE PRESS

Portland. The second Portland station of 1905 with staff posing on the curved platform; note the fine canopies and covered footbridge.

First published in 2001 by The Dovecote Press Ltd
Stanbridge, Wimborne, Dorset BH21 4JD

ISBN 1 874336 96 2

© Mike Oakley 2001

Mike Oakley has asserted his rights under the Copyright, Designs and Patent Act 1988 to be identified as author of this work

Series designed by Humphrey Stone

Typeset in Monotype Sabon
Printed and bound by Baskerville Press, Salisbury, Wiltshire

A CIP catalogue record for this book is available from the British Library

All rights reserved

1 3 5 7 9 8 6 4 2

CONTENTS

INTRODUCTION 8

THE STATIONS & HALTS 12 – 93

Abbotsbury – Ashley Heath Halt – Bailey Gate – Blandford
Boscombe – Bournemouth Central – Bournemouth West
Bradford Peverell & Stratton Halt – Branksome – Bridport
Bridport East Street – Bridport West Bay – Broadstone
Cattistock Halt – Charlton Marshall Halt – Chetnole Halt
Christchurch – Corfe Castle – Corfe Mullen Halt – Coryates Halt
Creekmoor Halt – Daggons Road – Dorchester South
Dorchester West – Easton – Evershot – Gillingham
Grimstone & Frampton – Hamworthy – Hamworthy Junction
Holton Heath – Lyme Regis – Maiden Newton – Melcombe Regis
Meyrick Park Halt – Monkton & Came Halt – Moreton
Parkstone – Pokesdown – Poole – Portesham – Portland
Powerstock – Radipole Halt – Rodwell
Sandsfoot Castle Halt – Sherborne – Shillingstone
Spetisbury Halt – Stalbridge – Stourpaine & Durweston Halt
Sturminster Newton – Swanage – Thornford Bridge Halt
Toller – Upwey – Upwey (Abbotsbury Branch)
Upwey Junction – Upwey Wishing Well Halt
Verwood – Wareham – Westham Halt – West Moors
Weymouth – Weymouth Quay – Wimborne – Wool
Wyke Regis Halt – Yetminster

FURTHER READING 94

ACKNOWLEDGEMENTS 95

Stations and Halts

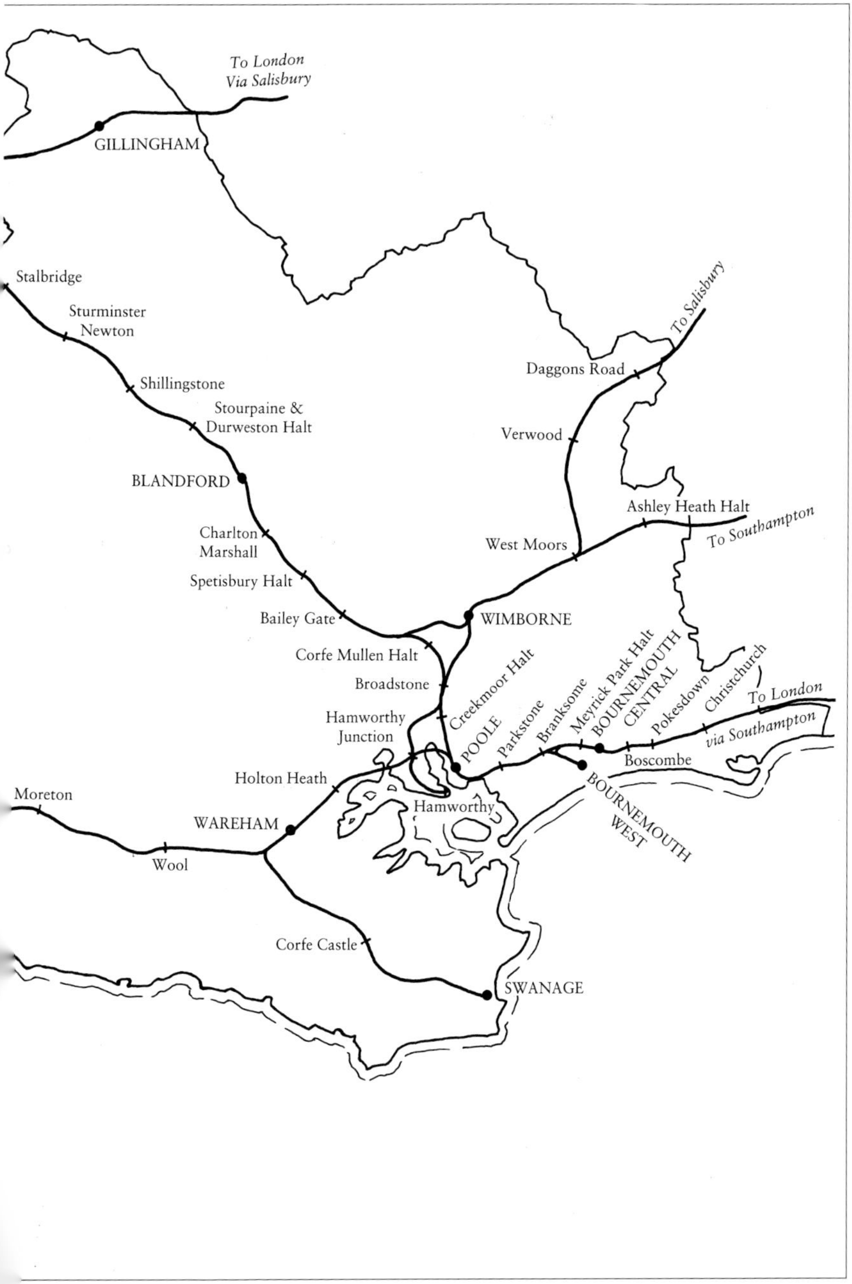
To London
Via Salisbury
GILLINGHAM
Stalbridge
Sturminster
Newton
Shillingstone
Stourpaine &
Durweston Halt
BLANDFORD
Charlton
Marshall
Spetisbury Halt
Bailey Gate
Corfe Mullen Halt
Broadstone
Hamworthy
Junction
Holton Heath
Moreton
WAREHAM
Wool
Corfe Castle
SWANAGE
Hamworthy
POOLE
Creekmoor Halt
Parkstone
Branksome
Meyrick Park Halt
BOURNEMOUTH
CENTRAL
BOURNEMOUTH
WEST
Boscombe
Pokesdown
Christchurch
To London
via Southampton
WIMBORNE
West Moors
Ashley Heath Halt
To Southampton
Verwood
Daggons Road
To Salisbury

INTRODUCTION

Dorset's railway stations and halts add a unique chapter to the county's social and economic history. The building styles of the different railway companies, often adapted to reflect local conditions and materials, resulted in many railway related buildings becoming of considerable architectural interest in their own right. Until the advent of the motorcar, there can have been few people in Dorset who didn't know the layout and characteristics of their own local station or halt as well as the street or lane in which they lived.

Town and country stations became the focus of both passenger and freight movements. In a rural area, like Dorset, the coming of the railway and the subsequent expansion and reduction of the rail network had a marked impact on all aspects of life. Seaside resorts, such as Weymouth and Swanage, were much influenced in their development by the arrival of the railway, as were a whole range of agricultural practices.

The area I have covered is that of the geographical county of Dorset in the year 2000. Thus stations and halts in the Bournemouth/ Christchurch area are included, but Yeovil Junction is not, due to county boundary changes. During the course of my research I have visited all Dorset's stations and halts (or the site where they once stood) generally over the period mid 1999 to mid 2000. I have travelled on all the current rail network in recent years; together with most of the earlier branch lines prior to their closure.

The accounts of each station and halt are in alphabetical order. The name of the station is generally that used in the late 1930s (except where it had already closed). Where the term 'Halt' is included in the title it can be assumed that no facilities for the handling of goods were ever provided. Where the terms 'up' and 'down' platforms are used, they refer to the platforms used for travel towards or away from London respectively. The photographs included are drawn from a large collection I have assembled from various sources over recent years. They have been selected primarily to illustrate significant and interesting features of the station or halt; thus only a few include locomotives or trains, as their presence in the photograph can obscure detail of the buildings!

THE DEVELOPMENT OF DORSET'S RAILWAY NETWORK 1847-1903

Dorset was a relative late-comer in entering the 'railway age' in the mid-nineteenth century. With a small population and little industrial or mining activity, the early promoters of railway schemes saw scant evidence of economic potential likely to produce them a revenue.

It is perhaps not surprising that Dorset's first railway was not primarily intended to serve the county itself but was part of a through route west into Devon and the rest of the South West. This line, the Southampton and Dorchester Railway, opened in 1847, and was seen as a key link in a new trunk route to the west. Joining the previously completed London and Southampton Railway, it provided the first through rail link from London into Dorset, running from Southampton through Ringwood, Wimborne and Wareham to Dorchester. Promoted by A.L. Castleman, a Wimborne solicitor, it was always accepted that significant volumes of local traffic would be difficult to generate. Thus its circuitous route was deliberately intended to serve as many towns as possible, giving the railway the nickname of 'Castleman's Corkscrew'. The planned continuation westwards from Dorchester never materialised and the through route role to the west was later taken by the Salisbury and Exeter Railway, which opened through north Dorset in 1859/1860, serving Gillingham and Sherborne.

The other significant early rail route in Dorset was the north/south Wilts, Somerset and Weymouth Railway, a subsidiary of the Great Western Railway, which opened within Dorset in 1857. A further north/south route followed six years later with the completion in 1863 of a line between Wimborne (where it branched from the Southampton and Dorchester Railway) and Templecombe in Somerset, where a link was established with the Salisbury and Exeter Railway in 1866. This through route via Blandford was in fact built in two stages: the first, by the Dorset Central Railway from Wimborne to just south of Blandford in 1860, and the second by the newly formed Somerset and Dorset Railway from Blandford north in 1863, which linked to the former Somerset Central Railway beyond Templecombe. The Dorset Central and Somerset Central Railways had amalgamated in September 1862 to become the well remembered Somerset and Dorset Railway.

The remainder of the railways in Dorset originated basically as a series of branch lines from the three main routes of Southampton to Dorchester, Yeovil to Weymouth and Salisbury to Exeter. Rather surprisingly this was the case in the Poole and Bournemouth area, the latter barely existing at the start of the railway age. Poole was first served by short branch lines to Hamworthy (1847) and then more directly to the town itself from Broadstone (1872), both lines branching from the Southampton to Dorchester Railway. The later branch was subsequently extended into the western side of Bournemouth in 1874. Some four years earlier the railway had penetrated into the east side of Bournemouth as an extension of the 1862 Ringwood to Christchurch line.

The year 1888 saw two significant developments: the opening of the direct line through the Bournemouth area linking the two earlier lines that had penetrated from the west and east and also, although not in Dorset, the opening of the direct route from Southampton to Bournemouth via Brockenhurst. This last replaced the longer route via Ringwood. The final piece in the railway jigsaw of the Poole/Bournemouth area was the opening of the Holes Bay curve in 1893, finally allowing the direct running of through services from London and Southampton into Dorset via Bournemouth and Poole, rather than via what was known as the 'old road' via Ringwood and Wimborne.

Other developments in the Dorset railway passenger network included Maiden Newton to Bridport (1857), Weymouth to Portland (1865), Wimborne to Salisbury (1866), Wareham to Swanage and the Abbotsbury branch (both 1885), Bridport to West Bay (1888), Weymouth Quay Tramway (1889), Portland to Easton (1902) and finally Axminster to Lyme Regis (1903). Apart from short lived branches to the military camps at Bovington and Blandford in the

Bournemouth Central. Arrival of a London train at the long down platform. A fine illustration of the high glazed roof (see page 18).

1920s, the Lyme Regis line was the last railway opened in the county.

There was generally little industry in Dorset to benefit from the development of this railway network over the period 1847-1903, but nevertheless the railways had a considerable impact on agricultural practice, in particular by encouraging a change from arable to dairy farming by providing fast and reliable transport for milk. The railway helped the market towns that were sited on the lines to grow at the expense of those that were not so fortunate. For coastal resorts such as Weymouth and Swanage the railway opened up the possibility of a few days by the sea for the thousands of factory workers of the industrial Midlands. Travel times to the capital were much reduced: for instance that between Dorchester and London was cut from fourteen hours by coach to four, and later, in the early twentieth century, to three hours (not significantly different from the time in the year 2001!).

THE STATIONS & HALTS

ABBOTSBURY

OPENED: 9th November 1885 (with the opening of the Abbotsbury Railway).

CLOSED: Passengers and goods – 1st December 1952 (with closure of the Abbotsbury branch).

A classic GWR branch line terminus, Abbotsbury Station stood, on a slight curve, on the south side of the line some quarter of a mile east of the village. The station building, designed as others on the branch line by William Clarke, was of yellowish stone with a distinctive roof of blue and red tiles alternating every third tile. The large canopy had a fretted valence, whilst a roof light helped illuminate the platform. The sole entry to the 275ft platform was via a gate adjacent to the west side of the building.

The main building, oil lit throughout its history, incorporated a ladies' room and toilets, gentlemen's toilets and a general waiting room through which access was gained to the booking hall. A short

Abbotsbury. Staff, passengers and autotrailer in about 1910.

Ashley Heath Halt. Train heading south towards Wimborne, 1963

siding behind the east end of the platform for a few years before the Second World War housed a GWR camping coach. Cattle pens and a goods shed (43 x 33ft) identical to that at Upwey stood on the south side of the line at the east end. The shed incorporated massive wooden sliding doors under a slate roof.

Unusually for a small branch line, Abbotsbury Station had two royal visits; most notably in 1904 the Prince and Princess of Wales visited the Fleet. In 1948 the station was the location setting for the film 'The Small Back Room'. For many years Abbotsbury was a popular destination for Sunday School trips from the Weymouth area, nearby fields being used for games and picnics. The station was also used for despatching large amounts of milk in churns.

In January 1963 the station building was demolished, the site being subsequently used for a new stone bungalow. The station approach road from the Portesham - Abbotsbury road is still in place leading towards the new bungalow. The original goods shed survives.

ASHLEY HEATH HALT

OPENED: 1st April 1927 (on the Southampton - Ringwood - Wimborne - Dorchester Railway, originally opened in 1847).

CLOSED: 4th May 1964 (with closure of the Ringwood - Broadstone line to passengers).

Opening nearly eighty years after the original Southampton - Dorchester Railway to serve the growing residential area to the west of Ringwood, the halt was on the west side of what was known as

Woolsbridge Crossing. A single public siding opened at the same time south east of the halt and was in use until 4th September 1961. Following closure, the track bed now forms part of the Castleman Trail path. The down platform has gone but part of the up platform remains in place together with the signboard, this having been restored by local residents in 1994.

BAILEY GATE

OPENED: 1st November 1860 (with the opening of the Wimborne - Blandford St Mary section of the Dorset Central Railway).

CLOSED: Passengers – 7th March 1966 (with closure of the Somerset and Dorset line, Poole to Bath Green Park, to passengers).
Goods – 5th April 1965 (milk traffic continued to be transported for a number of years).

The station stood in the meadows of the Stour valley, primarily to serve the village of Sturminster Marshall immediately to the north. Initially the station was called Sturminster Marshall, but in November 1863 it was renamed, apparently to avoid confusion with the newly opened (10th September 1863) Sturminster Newton Station. Nevertheless the relationship was reflected in the station name board 'Bailey Gate for Sturminster Marshall'. The station served not only local residents, but also developed considerable commercial traffic, in

Bailey Gate. Looking north west in July 1962 showing the down platform buildings and the goods yard serving the nearby dairy factory.

Blandford. The main buildings on the up platform and the tall 1893 signal box on the down platform in April 1965. (See also the Frontispiece).

particular dairy products from the adjacent United Dairies milk processing factory. There was also seasonal trade in watercress and mushrooms. The goods yard to the north of the station was expanded over the years to cope with the considerable milk/dairy traffic generated by United Dairies.

The station buildings were of basic Dorset Central Railway design; the brick buildings of the down platform incorporated the usual facilities and also a wooden porters' cabin. The up platform only had a small wooden shelter; the two platforms were linked via a timber foot crossing at the northern end.

For some twenty years after closure the platforms remained in place, though the track was lifted on 21st June 1970. The whole station site and goods yard is being redeveloped with industrial units, having been cleared in April 1992.

BLANDFORD

OPENED: Temporary station opened at Blandford St Mary 1st November 1860 (at the northern end of the Dorset Central Railway from Wimborne). Closed and replaced by the permanent Blandford Station on 10th September 1863 (with the opening of the Blandford St Mary - Blandford - Templecombe section of the now Somerset and Dorset Railway). A suffix 'Forum' was added to the station's name from 21st September 1953.

CLOSED: Passengers – 7th March 1966 (with closure of the Somerset and Dorset line, Poole to Bath Green Park, to passengers).
Goods – 13th February 1967 (some 'carted by public' traffic retained until final complete closure 6th January 1969).

The station stood close to the town centre and played a significant role in developing and strengthening Blandford's commercial status, particularly in the Victorian era. After 1927 an important function was serving pupils of the newly opened Bryanston School (hence the station sign 'Blandford Forum for Bryanston School'). It was also used by pupils travelling to and from Blandford Grammar School. Blandford Station acted for long periods as a significant arrival and departure point for the many troops serving in the nearby military camps, particularly during the two World Wars.

The station buildings, of Dorset Central design, were not only the largest but, in the view of many, the most impressive on the Somerset and Dorset Railway. The principal buildings were concentrated on the up platform, and were brick built with stone facing and a sizeable canopy. A canteen was located on this platform in the Second World War for use by the troops. The facilities on the slightly shorter down platform were, in comparison, modest and dominated by the tall 27 lever signal box opened in 1893, replacing an earlier box on the up platform. This second signal box was itself rebuilt in 1906 having been destroyed by fire started by lightning in a thunder storm on 23rd June of that year.

The platforms were connected by a subway; the only footbridge was a public structure not associated with the railway to the north of the station. To the north east of the station a large goods yard incorporated a goods shed, loading stage, cattle pens and a 7 ton crane.

The whole station site has now been developed for housing (Station Court); much of the goods yard is now a public car park (Station Court Car Park). The public footbridge remains north of the station's site and the station master's house continues in use (still appropriately named). A short section of railway line with a buffer stop is laid on the former track bed almost beneath the footbridge. A small section of track, originally in a goods yard siding, remains across the entrance to the car park and a locomotive wheel has also been erected.

BOSCOMBE

OPENED: 1st June 1897 (on the Christchurch to Bournemouth East line, originally opened in 1870).
CLOSED: Passengers – 4th October 1965.
Goods – 1st May 1972.

Boscombe Station opened following a long campaign by the local residents (see later text on Pokesdown). Located outside the two running tracks, the two platforms were covered by ornate canopies with glazed weather breaks at either end. The main buildings were surmounted by impressive chimneys; at the time of construction the station buildings represented an architectural style currently being developed by the London and South Western Railway.

The actual station site was, in late 1999, occupied by the Bournemouth Car Centre whilst the former goods yard to the south was a coal depot. The original entrance to the goods yard can be identified by the cobbled entrance at the corner of North Road.

Boscombe. The extensive station buildings with glazed wind shields and tall chimneys in 1963. Also note the large enclosed footbridge.

BOURNEMOUTH CENTRAL

OPENED: Original station – 18th March 1870 (as the terminus of the Ringwood - Christchurch - Bournemouth Railway).
Second station – 20th July 1885.

CLOSED: Passengers – remains open for services on the London (Waterloo) - Weymouth line.
Goods – 2nd July 1979.

In the mid 1840s Bournemouth was a small resort of some 500 residents. It was not an attractive prospect for rail promoters, and the chosen route for the new Southampton to Dorchester Railway, opening in 1847, by-passed Bournemouth to the north and west, serving instead the towns of Ringwood, Wimborne and Wareham, with a branch line to Hamworthy which also served Poole via a ferry and toll bridge. Thus in the late 1840s and 1850s travellers to Bournemouth could either alight at Holmesley (called Christchurch Road until 1863) on the Southampton to Dorchester Railway and then travel by coach, or alternatively could continue via the Hamworthy branch line and the ferry/toll bridge to Poole.

Bournemouth's first direct connection to the evolving rail network came with the opening in 1870 of a small station as the terminus of a single line section of the Ringwood, Christchurch and Bournemouth Railway, which had originally opened to Christchurch in 1862. This small terminus was only a single platform on the east side of Holdenhurst Road (ie on the other side of the road to the present station). Minimum shelter was provided. The suffix East was added to the name in 1874 with the opening of Bournemouth West Station.

With the accelerating expansion of the resort complaints increased, both about the poor facilities at Bournemouth East and also the inadequate rail services, particularly to London. To meet the latter concerns, new links were provided, including the direct route to Southampton via Brockenhurst and a new line linking the East and West stations, both in 1888.

The key element was the construction of a new station building, which started in April 1884 on a site west of Holdenhurst Road; from its opening in 1885 the original station (east of the road and separated by the 50 yard tunnel) was only used for goods traffic. The new

Bournemouth Central. The magnificent 'winter garden' interior in 1911.

station was designed to give the impression of a glass-roofed winter garden. It was built in red brick, the walls having buttresses surmounted by stone pediments. The buttresses took the thrust of twelve massive roof girders, each weighing some 17fi tons. The 95ft single span glazed roof at 40ft above platform level covered some 350 feet of the station platforms; the two main platforms were originally some 800 feet long (see also photograph on page 11).

Bournemouth Central. The imposing exterior of the down side with the original facade, canopy and now demolished covered main entrance.

Station facilities included a booking hall, refreshment room and waiting room on each platform; these were linked by a spacious well lit subway at the London end built with ramps for invalid chairs. Gas lighting was provided throughout and a portico covered each of the two main entrances.

The new station became Bournemouth Central as from 1st July 1893 and this suffix remained until 10th July 1967. Considerable developments and adaptations took place over the years, including the provision of a pedestrian bridge, which unfortunately interrupted the impressive view through the station.

Although a prestigious development in its early days the intricate details, and in particular the high glazed roof, created significant maintenance problems. Plans were put forward in the 1980s for demolition of what was now a listed building but these were refused. The severe 1990 gale caused major damage, particularly to the roof, and then for some years the whole station was a very depressing sight. Funding finally became available in the late 1990s and the revamped station, restored to its original splendour, was completed in 2000, the roof alone having been rebuilt at a cost of over £6 million.

BOURNEMOUTH WEST

OPENED: 15th June 1874 (as the terminus of the LSWR branch line from Poole).

CLOSED: Passengers and goods – 4th October 1965 (with closure of the line to Bournemouth West).

Bournemouth West Station opened in 1874 as the terminus of the single track branch line from Poole. Initially it comprised two converted cottages and a single platform; further buildings were added in the following year.

In 1888 the station buildings were united and extended to form a significant complex. The buildings faced south and, unusually for a terminus station, were not at right angles across the end of the tracks but parallel to them. The new station had six platforms, each with extensive canopies, but there was no overall roof. The two longest platforms were in the centre. Platform 4, housing the station master's office and a refreshment room, was the longest, but even it only just

Bournemouth West. The south facing terminus complex in the 1910s sited parallel to the rail tracks.

accommodated the 'Bournemouth Belle' express train to London Waterloo which for many years started from the station.

Throughout its life Bournemouth West was the terminus not only for trains from London but also from the Midlands and the North via the Somerset and Dorset line, including the famous 'Pines Express' from Manchester to Bournemouth. The death knell for the station came with the electrification of the line to London Waterloo and all passenger services to Bournemouth West ceased in October 1965.

The station buildings were subsequently demolished; much of the site is now occupied by the Wessex Way road (A35 bypass). The remainder is in use as a coach and car park. The adjacent, appropriately named, Midland Hotel survives.

BRADFORD PEVERELL AND STRATTON HALT

OPENED: 22nd May 1933 (on the Yeovil - Weymouth section of the Wilts, Somerset and Weymouth Railway (GWR), originally opened in 1857).
CLOSED: 3rd October 1966.

Serving the villages of Bradford Peverell to the south west and Stratton to the north west, this halt close to the A37 originally comprised two staggered wooden platforms, 150 ft long with shelters. The estimated cost was £575. These were replaced with pre-cast concrete components in 1959. Today both platforms survive reasonably intact, albeit overgrown.

BRANKSOME

OPENED: 1st June 1893 (on the Poole - Bournemouth direct railway, originally opened in 1888). Passenger station only.
CLOSED: remains open for passenger services on the London (Waterloo) to Weymouth line.

A late addition to the Bournemouth facilities, Branksome Station served the developing western suburbs of the growing town. Originally planned but not developed as an island platform similar to the first station at Pokesdown, Branksome Station was built as a

Bradford Peverell and Stratton Halt. The two staggered platforms, 1963.

Branksome. A view north west on 15th July 2000 showing the reduced canopies. The original booking hall is seen above the right canopy.

conventional brick-built LSWR station with two outer platforms covered with extensive canopies and linked by a covered footbridge. The booking hall, entrance and small parcels office, at ground level, led to a footbridge with steps leading down to the two platforms. An early name board on the platforms stated 'Branksome for Eastern Poole'.

In 1987 the platform canopies were cut back but three stanchions were retained on each platform and the roof repaired. A short canopy now remains in place on both platforms. The former booking hall is now called 'Rail Lodge'; the Branksome Station Hotel stands nearby.

BRIDPORT

OPENED: 12th November 1857 (with the opening of the Bridport Railway from Maiden Newton to Bridport).

CLOSED: Passengers – 5th May 1975 (with closure of the Bridport line).

Goods – 5th April 1965.

The coming of the railway in 1857 revolutionised life in west Dorset. The roads in the area were poor, even by normal mid nineteenth century standards, and the railway had a significant impact on both travel and trade. Raw materials for the town's net and twine factories

Bridport. Looking north, the up platform with long canopy, down platform with shelter, and small dock siding (left) in the 1920s

could be brought in more easily and the finished products taken out. The station also became a focal point for milk traffic, with milk being delivered by road to the station in churns and then dispatched either to other parts of the country or to a large dairy near Maiden Newton.

A significant drawback for the station was its location a mile from the town centre on the road to Bradpole. From 1887 to 1902 it was known locally as Bradpole Road Station to distinguish it from the more recently opened Bridport East Street and Bridport West Bay Stations; the name reverted to Bridport in 1902.

The original 1857 station was a stone built terminus with two platforms under a covering train shed. This initial alignment of the main station buildings continued throughout its life despite subsequent changes, in particular, the extension to West Bay. The tender for the initial construction was some £1,300.

The opening day was a public holiday in Bridport and most shops remained closed. The opening coincided with Yeovil Fair, which many townsfolk visited on the new train service, adding to the festive air.

The new single line extension to West Bay of 1884 meant that significant changes were necessary at Bridport Station. One track under the train shed was removed to allow the other to be slewed into a new curve leading into the extension. The platform face was rebuilt and curved to the revised alignment. On the March opening day of the

Bridport East Street. A 1905 view showing the stationmaster's house and station building both built in the previous year.

extension there was once again a carnival atmosphere, with most of the shops closing. In 1915, despite difficulties associated with the First World War, the station was awarded a £5 prize as the best kept station in the Westbury District of the Great Western Railway.

All traces of the station have been obliterated by the diversion of the Bridport to Bradpole road through the site. However a small row of cottages originally associated with the station remains, together with a short section of wall alongside the original alignment of the road.

BRIDPORT EAST STREET

OPENED: 31st March 1884 (with the opening of the West Bay extension of the Bridport Railway). Passenger station only.

CLOSED: 22nd September 1930 (temporary closure, 31st December 1915 - 7th July 1919).

East Street Station was sited close to the centre of Bridport at the eastern end of East Street. In order to save money, a nearby thatched cottage was purchased and converted into station master's accommodation, a booking office and waiting room. On the opening day an archway decorated with flags and greenery was erected near the station over East Street, on one side was a scroll stating 'Success to the Railway' and on the other 'Prosperity to West Bay'.

Bridport West Bay. A branch line train in 1906. Note the fretted canopy and oil lamps one of which is being tended in the distance.

Passengers wishing to shelter from the weather had to wait in the slightly distant station buildings which were re-thatched in 1885. Following complaints, in July 1889 a waiting room was erected on the platform itself at a cost of £15. In 1893 a cast iron gent's toilet was also erected.

In 1904, after the take over of the Bridport Railway by the Great Western Railway, the thatched station building, the waiting room and toilet on the platform were removed. A new brick building of standard Great Western design was constructed on the platform together with a new station master's house. All traces of the station have now gone and road improvements have obliterated all signs of the railway.

BRIDPORT WEST BAY

OPENED: 31st March 1884 (with the opening of the West Bay extension of the Bridport Railway).

CLOSED: Passengers – 22nd September 1930 (temporary closure 31st December 1915 - 7th July 1919).
Goods – 3rd December 1962 (very limited subsequent use for movement of coal and shingle until 1st January 1966).

Development of this station was linked with the anticipated expansion of West Bay as a holiday resort. Over the years the importance of Bridport harbour as a commercial port had declined. The opening of the railway to the town in 1857 had resulted in many goods hitherto coming in by sea now arriving by train.

The new terminal station, of stone construction to a design common all over the Great Western Railway system, was first named Bridport Harbour but was renamed West Bay shortly after the line's opening as part of the plan to develop the area as a resort.

Despite the early optimism, by the late 1920s West Bay had still not really developed; only speculative and isolated buildings had been built. In the summer of 1933 a camping coach was sited at the closed station, an eight berth coach fully equipped with bed linen, cutlery and crockery. This was withdrawn at the outbreak of the Second World War.

Although it served its last regular passengers as long ago as September 1930 the main station building has remained in reasonable condition. In the late 1990s the building was extensively restored, two railway coaches were placed on track beside the platform and the former station took on a new role as a West Dorset District Council Information Centre.

BROADSTONE

OPENED: 1st June 1847 (with the opening of the Southampton - Ringwood - Wimborne - Dorchester Railway).

CLOSED: Passengers – 7th March 1966 (with the closure of the Bath Green Park - Poole line).

Goods – 20th September 1965 (some 'carted by public' traffic retained until final closure 7th March 1966).

Originally opened to serve passengers and freight on the Southampton to Dorchester Railway in 1847, the station assumed greater importance as a junction with the opening of the branch line to Poole on 2nd December 1872. Further traffic came with the opening in 1886 of the Corfe Mullen to Broadstone cut off route, which served to by-pass Wimborne for much of the north/south traffic on the Somerset and Dorset line. With so many changes of function, the station's name

Broadstone. The deserted station looking south on
22nd September 1963

changed seven times, more than any other station in Dorset.

Although nearby housing and new residential estates generated some passenger traffic (including school pupils), the principal role of the station was as a junction. Between the arrival and departure of long distance trains, the four platforms were virtually deserted.

Nothing now remains, the whole station site having been redeveloped with the Broadstone Leisure Centre's indoor and outdoor facilities. Its original use is commemorated in the 'Castleman Trail', which passes alongside the Leisure Centre, and also in the road name 'Station Approach'. The original Railway Hotel near the station has been renamed 'The Broadstone Hotel'.

CATTISTOCK HALT

OPENED: 3rd August 1931 (on the Yeovil - Weymouth section of the Wilts, Somerset and Weymouth Railway (GWR), originally opened in 1857.

CLOSED: 3rd October 1966.

The original timber built two platform halt with shelters and paraffin vapour lighting was constructed at an estimated cost of £636. The two platforms were rebuilt with concrete pre-cast sections in 1959. After closure the two platforms were re-used for single platforms at Chetnole and Thornford. All remains of the halt have gone.

Cattistock Halt. The re-built halt looking north on 18th April 1964

Charlton Marshall Halt. Looking north in April 1965, after closure.

CHARLTON MARSHALL HALT

OPENED: 9th July 1928 (on the Wimborne - Blandford St Mary section of the Dorset Central Railway, originally opened 1860).

CLOSED: 17th September 1956, but nevertheless continued to be used until 17th December 1963 by pupils at the nearby Claysmore School at the beginning and end of each term.

A very basic late addition for passengers on the Somerset and Dorset Railway, the halt had no shelters on either platform. These were connected via steps and a road bridge. Both platforms were short and could accommodate little more than a locomotive and one or two coaches. The platforms remain in reasonable condition and are both accessed by refurbished steps currently used by walkers to gain access to the old trackbed which now forms part of the Stour Valley Way. The station signboard is preserved at the 7/ inch gauge Moors Railway at West Moors.

Chetnole Halt. The two wooden platforms divided by a road bridge, 1962.

CHETNOLE HALT

OPENED: 11th September 1933 (on the Yeovil - Weymouth section of the Wilts, Somerset and Weymouth Railway (GWR), originally opened in 1857).

CLOSED: remains open for passenger services on the Bristol - Weymouth line. Trains stop by request only.

From its opening the halt, costing £410, comprised two oil lit staggered timber platforms (each 150ft x 7fift) on the double track line. They were separated by a road overbridge from which steps led down to both platforms (up platform north of the bridge and down platform south).

The original wooden up platform was replaced by a redundant concrete platform and shelter from the former Cattistock Halt when this closed in 1966. With singling of the line on 26th May 1968, the down platform was demolished.

CHRISTCHURCH

OPENED: First station – 13th November 1862 as the terminus of the first section of the Ringwood - Christchurch - Bournemouth branch line.
Second station – 30th May 1886 (with the doubling of the line to Bournemouth East).

Christchurch. Looking west towards Bournemouth early in the 1900s.

CLOSED: Passengers – remains open for services on the London (Waterloo) to Weymouth line.
Goods – 1st May 1972.

The original 1862 Christchurch terminus station fulfilled an early role until 1870 as the first rail facility for the developing town of Bournemouth. The single track branch line was then extended west to the new terminus at Bournemouth East, giving 'valuable impetus to the new watering place of Bournemouth'. The original Christchurch Station buildings were to the east of the current road bridge and are today the site of modern industrial buildings.

A new station, upon which work commenced in October 1885, was opened in May 1886 in association with the doubling of the line to Bournemouth East. The main entrance on the down side and the two platforms, with extensive canopies, were linked by a covered footbridge.

No significant alterations have been made to the 1886 buildings and they are currently in good condition following refurbishment, though the footbridge roof has been removed.

CORFE CASTLE

OPENED: 20th May 1885 (with the opening of the Wareham - Swanage Railway).
CLOSED: Passengers – 3rd January 1972 (with closure of Swanage branch line)
Goods – 4th October 1965.
REOPENED: Passengers – 12th August 1995 (on the restored Swanage Railway).

Sited close to the village centre and the famous castle, the opening of the station in 1885 greatly added to the number of visitors. Until the motor car era the railway was the principal means of access to the village, and the station served the whole of the Isle of Purbeck.

The attractive LSWR main station building, on the up side, is constructed of Purbeck stone and roofed with red tiles. The main entrance led through the booking hall to the platforms; the ticket office separated the booking hall from the adjacent station master's two storey house. No bridge was ever built between the platforms and access to the down platform was via foot boards across the tracks at the Swanage end. Accommodation on the down side platform comprised only a basic waiting shelter.

Corfe Castle. From the Swanage end with goods shed (left), main buildings (centre left) and down platform shelter (right). Note crossing footboards.

Corfe Mullen Halt. The short platform with a basic shelter.

A feature of the station, for some years, was a pair of camping coaches at the Swanage end of the down platform; a converted Pullman coach also appeared in about 1968. On the up side of the station site was a small goods shed with two small awnings on either side.

Corfe Castle Station has now been restored to much of its former splendour with its reopening on the Swanage Railway. In particular much of the interior has been renovated, incorporating some fittings taken from other former London and South Western Railway stations.

CORFE MULLEN HALT

OPENED: 27th June 1928 (on the Corfe Mullen - Broadstone cut off single line, originally opened for goods traffic in 1885 and passenger traffic in 1886).

CLOSED: 17th September 1956.

The residents of Corfe Mullen campaigned for a halt to be provided from the time of the cut off line opening. The facilities were basic with a small shelter and only one gas lamp providing illumination to the short platform. The cutting in which the halt stood was filled during the 1980s, the actual site being now beneath the grounds of 112 Wimborne Road. The former railway alignment continues on the north west side of the Corfe Mullen - Wimborne road along the now appropriately named 'Corfe Halt Close'.

Coryates Halt. A 1952 photograph showing the cut out section on the right of the building for milk churn storage.

CORYATES HALT

OPENED: 1st May 1906 (on the Abbotsbury branch line, originally opened in 1885).

CLOSED: 1st December 1952 (with closure of the branch line).

When originally built on its embankment site, the halt comprised a platform 100ft long, 7ft wide, and only 14in above the rail level; lamps and a name board were provided but no shelter. Passengers had to use folding steps to access the train. In 1907 the platform was raised to a height of three feet and a waiting shelter provided at a cost of £56. In later years the shelter was cut away at the Abbotsbury end so that milk churns could be placed in the shade. Patronage was always very limited though the halt was sometimes the destination for excursion trips. No trace of the halt now remains.

CREEKMOOR HALT

OPENED: 19th June 1933 (on the Broadstone - Poole line, originally opened in 1872).

CLOSED: 7th March 1966 (with closure of Bath Green Park - Poole line).

Creekmoor Halt. Train from Wimborne in 1963 under the footbridge

Initially built to serve the developing Creekmoor and Waterloo communities, the halt's original platforms, constructed of old wooden sleepers, were only the length of 2 or 3 coaches. To serve the nearby RAF factory the wooden platforms were replaced and extended early in the Second World War. Only the original waiting shelters of corrugated metal (down) and wood (up) were retained. A small wooden hut served as a ticket office. Initially there was no footbridge, but a 'southern' type concrete bridge was later provided. The whole site is now covered by industrial development.

DAGGONS ROAD

OPENED: 1st January 1876 (on the Salisbury and Dorset Junction Railway, originally opened 20th December 1866).

CLOSED: Passengers and goods – 4th May 1964 (with closure of the original Salisbury and Dorset Junction Line).

The station served both Daggons Road and Alderholt, after which it

Daggons Road. The 9.23 Salisbury to Bournemouth West on the last day of passenger services; also showing booking office and ladies' room.

was initially named for five months until May 1876. The main buildings were sited on the up platform (towards Salisbury) including a booking office, ladies' room and a station master's house, but no platform canopy.

The station master's house remains in use as a private residence; other buildings have gone. The original road bridge to the south of, and adjacent to, the station has been removed and the road straightened; the former access road to the goods yard on the eastern side is still named 'Station Yard'.

DORCHESTER SOUTH

OPENED: 1st June 1847 (as the western terminus of the Southampton - Dorchester Railway).

CLOSED: Passengers – remains open for services on the London (Waterloo) - Weymouth line.
Goods – 1st March 1965 (with the concentration of goods traffic at Weymouth, though some 'carted by public' traffic was retained until 1st December 1980).

At its opening the station layout, with the line leading westwards and

Dorchester South. The up platform (right), the original down platform (centre) and the 1879 curved down platform (left). The timber built train shed (centre) covers the straight tracks and the short down platform.

not towards Weymouth, reflected the Southampton and Dorchester Railway's ambition to extend the line along the coast to Bridport and Exeter. This extension was strongly opposed both by local residents and also by the Great Western Railway, which ten years later, through its subsidiary the Wilts, Somerset and Weymouth Railway, effectively cut the route westward by opening its line from Yeovil via Dorchester to Weymouth. From this new north/south line came a spur back to the Southampton and Dorchester Railway station.

A single long platform with a cross over facility at the mid point initially served both up and down trains, a common arrangement when the town was principally on one side of the station. Later a second shorter platform parallel to the original platform was opened, primarily to serve down trains. With these arrangements through up and down trains serving Weymouth had to undertake reversing movements to gain access to the two platforms.

Following the doubling of the Weymouth spur in 1878, a new down platform was constructed on the inside of the spur curve and brought into use in 1879, thus making the former additional down platform redundant. A subway was later built to link the new curved down platform with the original up platform. This revised arrangement meant that the up trains from Weymouth still had to perform a reversing movement.

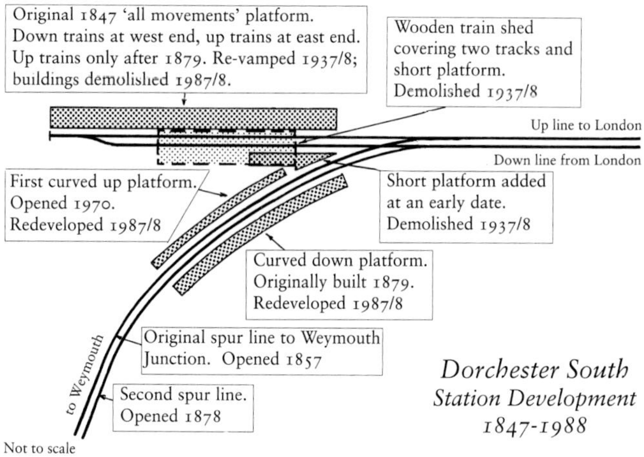

Dorchester South
Station Development
1847-1988

A timber built train shed covered the original lines and the subsequent short down platform, with a heavy wooden canopy over the up platform. The 1879 curved down platform was provided with timber buildings incorporating waiting room accommodation and toilets. In 1937/1938 the old train shed and the short down platform were removed; a new canopy was provided for the main station building, which at the same time was given a general face lift.

In 1970 came a further major change with the erection of a new up platform with a waiting room, shelter and canopy on the outside of the Weymouth link curve. However, the principal buildings on the old up platform remained in use and thus an elevated link walkway was constructed across the old trackbed.

Over the years some twenty five railway associated buildings were constructed in and around the station area to accommodate all the railway staff, including a large station master's house. The main station buildings were well built in brick with projecting stone pillars at intervals and at the corners. Unfortunately the most interesting of the other railway buildings, a lodge at the station entrance, together with a row of six cottages in the approach road, were demolished in association with the 1986 multi million pound redevelopment scheme agreed between British Railways and Eldridge Pope, the brewers.

A new station building was constructed on the site of the 1970 built

Dorchester West. Looking north in about 1930 showing the wooden roof which covered both platforms for many years, demolished in 1934.

curved up platform; incorporating a waiting room, booking office, toilets and a separate shelter, coming into use on 21st November 1987. Soon afterwards the old station building was demolished and the site together with the goods yard was taken over by the brewery's bottling and distribution depot. The old curved down platform of 1879 was rebuilt and a new footbridge constructed. The former station master's house was refurbished and opened as a public house on 18th July 1989.

DORCHESTER WEST

OPENED: 20th January 1857 (with the opening of the Yeovil - Weymouth section of the Wilts, Somerset and Weymouth Railway (GWR)).

CLOSED: Passengers – remains open for services on the Bristol - Weymouth line.
Goods – 1st March 1965 (coal traffic retained until 6th September 1965).

A fine station built in the style of the Wilts, Somerset and Weymouth Railway (GWR), it was designed by the architect Ritson. The main buildings, on the down side, were constructed of rendered stone under a broad hipped roof and deep eaves. They incorporated round headed

Dorchester West. Looking north in about 1950 showing the fine platform canopies that replaced the overall roof in the mid 1930s.

windows. First and second class passengers were provided with separate waiting rooms; there was also a first class ladies' room and gentlemen's toilets. For some years a Wyman's bookstall also served passengers on the down platform.

The original buildings on the up platform, linked to the down platform by a footbridge, were rather limited. To serve increased passenger traffic, a new brick built building was constructed in the early twentieth century, providing a waiting room, ladies' waiting room with toilets and a gent's urinal. A small kink in the up platform edge ensured clearance for locomotives using the track crossover. In 1908 both platforms were extended northwards by 160 ft and the down platform was also widened.

A particular feature of the station from its early years was a fine wooden overall roof strengthened with iron trusses covering both platforms. This was removed in 1934 and replaced by glazed canopies on both platforms.

The scale of operations at Dorchester West in the 1940s can be judged by the number of staff involved: they included two booking clerks, a platform foreman, two lady ticket collectors, a leading parcels porter, two parcel porters and three platform porters.

Extensive goods facilities developed over the years, in particular to the south of the station on the down side. They included the former broad gauge stone built goods shed (a feature of the station site for many years), traders' sidings and cattle pens. Just as with passengers, there was competition for freight traffic with the Dorchester South Station; the latter eventually took over as the leading goods station because of its better links with the London area.

The station became unstaffed as from January 1972; the buildings on the up platform were demolished and replaced by a small brick shelter. The basic structure of the original station remains on the down side; being 'listed' it is unlikely to be demolished. The footbridge and many of the railings remain as built; overall it is judged to be the best surviving example of Wilts, Somerset and Weymouth Railway (GWR) architecture. No rooms remain open for rail passenger use, the surviving building being currently used as a restaurant.

EASTON

OPENED: Passengers – 1st September 1902 .
Goods – 1st October 1900 (as the terminus of the new Easton and Church Hope Railway).

CLOSED: Passengers – 1st March 1952 (with closure of the Weymouth - Portland - Easton line to passenger traffic).
Goods – 5th April 1965.

The original 1902 station located west of, and close to, the centre of Easton in a sheltered cutting was described at its opening as 'a single platform 300 ft long, a loop line for engines to change ends, a goods

Easton. Staff pose in front of the buildings re-built after the 1903 fire.

yard and sidings'. The main local stone building incorporated a booking hall, a general waiting room, a ladies' room and toilets for both sexes. A small goods shed was also provided in the goods yard. A single track small engine shed came into use from 6th February 1905.

The original station building was largely destroyed by fire on 28th November 1903, but was rebuilt in the original form between May and September 1904. For some years a good collection of fossils was exhibited on the platform, collected from the railway cutting and nearby quarries, whilst further items were displayed in glass fronted cases inside the station.

Passenger services to Easton ceased as a wartime measure from 11th November 1940, although summer services ran over the period 1941-1944. Regular services recommenced on 1st January 1945. Following closure of the station to passengers in 1952, the building remained for some years but without its canopy. Following demolition the site was taken over in December 1972 by the local council and redeveloped for the Ladymead Elderly Persons Home.

EVERSHOT

OPENED: 20th January 1857 (with the opening of the Yeovil - Weymouth section of the Wilts, Somerset and Weymouth Railway (GWR)).

CLOSED: Passengers – 3rd October 1966
Goods – 7th September 1964.

This rather remote station was actually at Holywell, little more than a cross roads and a group of houses (including a row of cottages associated with the railway) and a long walk from Evershot village to the west. An unusual feature was that Lord and Lady Ilchester had the right to have any passenger train stop at the station, either by themselves in person or by an order signed by themselves.

The station was unusual on the original Wilts, Somerset and Weymouth line in being constructed of timber rather than stone; the main buildings standing on the up platform. A footbridge connected the two platforms and in the early days was covered by an ornate roof canopy. The station was immaculately kept and was known for its

Evershot. Staff and passengers in front of the
attractive wooden building on the up platform.

rambling roses and other climbing plants.

A goods yard was sited on the up side; cattle pens were served by a small siding behind the up platform. Alterations took place to the station over the years, including lengthening the platforms in 1913/14. Up until the mid 1940s Evershot had its own station master; during the 1950s staff at Evershot comprised two porters and three signal men. It became unstaffed as from 7th September 1964 when goods facilities were withdrawn. Following demolition in 1967 little remains to be seen apart from isolated railings and posts. The row of railway cottages to the south west of the station remains.

GILLINGHAM

OPENED: 2nd May 1859 (as a temporary terminus of the Salisbury - Yeovil - Exeter Railway).

CLOSED: Passengers – remains open for services on the London (Waterloo) - Exeter line.
Goods – 5th April 1965.

Following a number of abortive schemes for links to the national rail network, the Salisbury and Yeovil Railway Company was formed and

Gillingham. A fine view early in the 20th century of a Yeovil bound train and the impressive William Tite designed building on the up platform.

the first sod for the line's construction was turned on 3rd August 1856. The ceremony took place at Chantry Field, Gillingham at the entrance to which an ornate arch was decked with the flags of England, France, Sardinia and Turkey - our unlikely allies in the Crimean War, which had ended earlier that year.

The main station building, opened in 1859, was, and continues to be a notable example of the architecture of Sir William Tite. The substantial buildings on the up line included slate hung walls to keep out the damp; the slates were later removed. A brick shelter was provided on the down platform. Surprisingly, unlike the less used stations further east the footbridge was never roofed; the steel span and brick approach to the footbridge were removed in 1967 and replaced by an all concrete structure moved from Dinton Station in Wiltshire.

The original station buildings remain largely unaltered. For some years the station nameboard announced 'Gillingham for Mere' as the London and South Western Railway also ran the bus service to Mere.

OPENED: Passengers – 20th January 1857 (with the opening of the Yeovil - Weymouth section of the Wilts, Somerset and Weymouth Railway (GWR)).
Goods – October 1905.
CLOSED: Passengers – 3rd October 1966.
Goods – 1st May 1961.

Sited on an embankment on the side of the Frome valley, the station served the villages of Grimstone to the south west and Frampton to the north west. Opening with the line in 1857 it was named Frampton at the outset, with the name subsequently changing to Grimstone in July 1857 and finally Grimstone and Frampton from July 1858. From doubling of the track in the mid 1880s the station comprised two platforms connected by a footbridge. The brick station buildings included the main offices plus parcels facilities and a gents' toilet on the down platform and a waiting shelter on the up platform. Fine ornate lamps were provided on both platforms. The station became un-staffed as from 11th April 1966.

Goods facilities were not provided until 1905. As in many country stations, coal that had arrived by train for the local traders was delivered by the local pick up truck. The station was demolished in 1967, but some traces of the base of the platform and buildings remain, particularly on the down side.

Grimstone and Frampton. Looking north.

OPENED: 1st June 1847 (as the southern terminus of the Poole Junction - Poole branch line from the Southampton - Dorchester Railway).

CLOSED: Passengers – 1st July 1896 (with closure of Hamworthy branch line for passenger services).
Goods – 2nd March 1981 (date of formal closure for goods traffic though the branch line continues in use for limited freight traffic).

This first 1847 Poole Station (name changed to Hamworthy 2nd December 1872), from which passengers travelled on to the town by a toll bridge or ferry, only had a short life, declining in importance with the opening of the direct branch line from Broadstone to Poole in 1872. Passenger trains were finally withdrawn as from 1st July 1896. The branch line continues in use for freight traffic serving the harbour and private sidings. The original station building has now been demolished but a later brick extension remains behind the remnants of the original platform.

Hamworthy. The old Southampton and Dorchester Railway building on the original down platform in about 1900.

Hamworthy Junction. Looking east towards Poole on 16th March 1963, the platforms then covered by extensive awnings.

HAMWORTHY JUNCTION

OPENED: 1st June 1847 (at the junction of the Southampton - Dorchester Railway and the branch line to the first Poole station).

CLOSED: Passengers – remains open for services on the London (Waterloo) - Weymouth line.
Goods – 20th September 1965.

The first station opened as Poole Junction (re-named Hamworthy Junction 2nd December 1872) at the point where the branch line led southwards away from the main Southampton to Dorchester railway to the first Poole Station (re-named Hamworthy in 1872). The original buildings were demolished in 1892 and a new station opened at the same time as the Holes Bay curve in 1893. An island down platform became available for use with the Holes Bay curve; in 1901 the branch platform became a loop line. The down platform buildings on the island platform, including a waiting room, were originally covered with an extensive awning.

These buildings were replaced in 1972 by a 'bus shelter' with a flat roof. The original principal up side brick buildings of 1892 remain in place but in rather poor condition with a shortened canopy. The platforms were, and still are, connected by a subway which also acts as a pedestrian link between two residential areas.

Holton Heath. Looking east towards Poole on 16th March 1963.

HOLTON HEATH

OPENED: 3rd April 1917 (on the Southampton - Dorchester Railway, originally opened in 1847). Passenger station only.
CLOSED: remains open for services on the London (Waterloo) - Weymouth line.

This small station near the west shore of Poole Harbour opened in 1917 for use by workers at the naval cordite works in operation from 1914 to 1961. The station became available for general public use as from 14th July 1924 but became unstaffed from 1st June 1964. The two platforms remain in use. Protection is currently provided by small shelters on each platform, which in recent years have replaced very utilitarian facilities. The original small footbridge remains.

LYME REGIS

OPENED: 24th August 1903 (with the opening of the Axminster and Lyme Regis Light Railway).
CLOSED: Passengers – 29th November 1965 (with closure of Lyme Regis branch line).
Goods – 3rd February 1964.

Lyme Regis Station was the coastal terminus of the last passenger railway line constructed in Dorset. The platform, with a bay, on the west side of the single line unfortunately had to be built some half a mile uphill from the town centre because immediately beyond the line's buffer stops the land falls steeply towards the sea. To mark the opening, flags and bunting were displayed at the station and throughout the town, church bells rang and the artillery band played.

The largely wooden station building featured an intricate and attractive fretted canopy edge. A northern extension of the building was initially used as a book stall but later as a store. The platform was reconstructed in the 1920s in Southern Railway days with a new SR style sign erected. This new sign omitted any reference to Charmouth, named for some years on a previous sign. By 1936 the book stall had lost its end windows and was later removed to St Mary Cray Station in Kent.

Following complete closure of the line in 1965 the station buildings lay derelict for over 14 years. Early in 1979 the Mid Hants Railway (the Watercress Line) removed much of the timber building, re-erecting it as a gift and book shop at Alresford. The whole site of Lyme Regis Station is currently occupied by a builders' merchant and light industrial units.

Lyme Regis. The station buildings in about 1910 including an attractive platform canopy with a fretted edge and a book stall at the northern end.

OPENED: 20th January 1857 (with the opening of the Yeovil - Weymouth section of the Wilts, Somerset and Weymouth Railway (GWR)).

CLOSED: Passengers – remains open for services on the Bristol - Weymouth line.

Goods – 5th April 1965 (some 'carted by public' facilities retained until final closure 18th April 1966).

In addition to serving both passenger and freight movements originating in the village itself and surrounding rural areas, Maiden Newton Station acted as a junction for the Bridport Railway, which opened on 12th November 1857. The original 1857 main line was single track with Maiden Newton a crossing point (as once again exists today after removal of the second track in 1968).

Following laying of the second track in the early 1880s, the station comprised two platforms serving the main line and a terminal bay for the use of branch line trains; the bay was provided with a timber built covered train shed demolished in the late 1960s. The knapped flint buildings included the main station facilities on the up platform, which was itself widened in 1913, and a waiting shelter on the down. For most of its life the two platforms were linked by a lattice framed bridge, but this was replaced by a Southern Region type concrete

Maiden Newton. Looking south towards Dorchester showing the partly covered Bridport branch bay platform.

structure from a closed station on the Salisbury - Exeter line.

Today the station is a far cry from the days before the Second World War when the staff comprised a station master, two porters, a lad porter, two shunters, three signal men, a parcel porter, a booking clerk and a junior clerk.

A goods shed and traders' sidings were located at the Dorchester end on the up side. Originally built for the broad gauge railway, the goods shed was constructed of stone, flint and timber. Freight traffic at the station between the wars, and up to the 1950s, consisted of coal and other goods for local merchants. Also of some significance was milk, passing through in churns, from the United Dairies plant at Powerstock.

The up side main building and the down platform shelter remain, together with the later concrete footbridge. The main building is used by an I.T. Training Centre. The branch line trackbed has been filled in but traces of the train shed remain, including a short flight of steps at the end closest to the main buildings. Considerable remnants of the railings and gates remain.

MELCOMBE REGIS

OPENED: 30th May 1909 (on the Weymouth - Portland Railway, originally opened on 16th October 1865). Passenger station only.
CLOSED: 3rd March 1952 (with closure of Weymouth - Portland line for passengers).

From the opening of the Weymouth to Portland Railway in 1865 train movements from Weymouth Station onto the Portland line involved reversal, as the junction with the main line, a short distance north of Weymouth Station, faced south.

In 1908 when it became necessary to replace the original 1864/1865 wooden railway viaduct over the Backwater, the opportunity was taken to build a separate branch line station, Melcombe Regis, on the embankment leading to the new viaduct.

It opened in 1909 and comprised a single platform some 400ft in length on the town side of the line. The building's first canopy was small but was later replaced by a larger structure. Distinctive features were the later large iron screen on the Backwater side of the line to

Melcombe Regis. Towards Weymouth on 7th June 1958 showing the iron protective shield, the tall chimneys and the later large platform canopy.

protect waiting passengers from the wind and a row of tank traps constructed during the Second World War.

Although formally closed in 1952, it remained in use as a regular relief platform for the main station until September 1965 and even occasionally thereafter. The station building was demolished in 1966. Remains of the concrete platform can still be seen at the side of a car park, adjacent to the road over the new Backwater bridge.

MEYRICK PARK HALT

OPENED: 1st March 1906 (on the Bournemouth - Poole direct line, originally opened in 1888).

CLOSED: 1st November 1917.

Opened FL of a mile west of Bournemouth Central Station for what was then a growing residential area, the halt was mainly served by local steam rail-motor services. It closed as a First World War economy measure in 1917 and never reopened. No trace can now be seen.

MONKTON AND CAME HALT

OPENED: 1st July 1905 (on the Dorchester - Weymouth section of the Wilts, Somerset and Weymouth Railway (GWR), originally opened 20th January 1857).

CLOSED: 7th January 1957.

The two platform timber-built halt opened following the introduction

Meyrick Park Halt. The only known photograph of this small halt.

of local steam rail-motor services between Dorchester and Weymouth, principally to serve golfers at the nearby club on Came Down (the original name was Came Bridge Halt). The halt was of use to the residents of the nearby Winterborne Monkton and was re-named Monkton and Came Halt as from 1st October 1905. The platforms were at a later date rebuilt from concrete components. No shelters were ever provided but there was limited lighting with oil lamps. The halt closed in 1957; remains of the two platforms can still be seen on both sides of the line.

Monkton and Came Halt. The disused platforms looking north, 1963.

MORETON

OPENED: 1st June 1847 (with the opening of the Southampton - Dorchester Railway).

CLOSED: Passengers – remains open for services on the London (Waterloo) - Weymouth line.
Goods – 1st March 1965, though coal traffic was retained until 20th September 1965.

Opening with the Southampton to Dorchester Railway in 1847, Moreton Station is over a mile from the village. The principal buildings were originally on the up side, and incorporated an impressive gable and intricate canopy. The original down side shelter was of unusual design, with elliptical arches facing the tracks. Through the years a series of ad hoc extensions were made to the principal up side building; these included uses relating to the adjacent small goods yard.

The platforms were first extended in 1970 to take four car units and again in 1988 with the arrival of the new South Wessex electric trains. Moreton Station became unstaffed as from 1st March 1965.

The original buildings on both platforms have been replaced by small bus shelter type facilities. The nearby public house, 'The Frampton Arms', houses a series of souvenirs and pictures, both of the station itself and of other railways.

Moreton. Looking east in February 1964 showing main buildings on the up platform (left) and a substantial wooden shelter on the down (right).

PARKSTONE

OPENED: 15th June 1874 (with the opening of the Poole - Bournemouth West extension of the original Broadstone - Poole branch line).

CLOSED: Passengers – remains open for services on the London (Waterloo) - Weymouth line.
Goods – 20th September 1965 (date of final closure though much of the goods traffic was transferred to Poole Station in about 1953).

Parkstone Station was the only intermediate station when the London and South Western Railway Broadstone to Poole branch line was extended to Bournemouth West in 1874. From modest early buildings, a significant suburban station developed. The principal buildings, on the up-side, included the station master's house and, at one time, a W.H.Smith bookstall. Facilities on the down side comprised a substantial wooden shelter and a gent's toilet. Both the up and down platform buildings were originally provided with canopies, though of different designs, indicating varied dates of construction. A fully glazed footbridge was provided in 1888. The station's role was illustrated in the name board 'Parkstone for Sandbanks', a residential area two miles to the south.

Houses were built on the small former goods yard after its closure

Parkstone. A view east towards Bournemouth on 16th March 1963, the footbridge has lost its roof and glazing

Pokesdown. An early photograph of the first station with the buildings on an island platform between the then two tracks.

in 1965. The main up platform buildings are still in place linked by the now uncovered bridge (roof and glazing removed in the early 1950s) to the down platform which is now only provided with a bus shelter type facility, the original buildings having been demolished.

POKESDOWN

OPENED: 1st July 1886 (on the Christchurch - Bournemouth East extension of the Ringwood - Christchurch line, originally opened in 1870). Passenger station only.

CLOSED: remains open for passenger services on the London (Waterloo) - Weymouth line.

The first 1886 Pokesdown Station, built after a long campaign by residents in the Boscombe/Pokesdown area, was not ideally sited in a deep cutting. Estimated to have cost some £2000, the station entrance on the road bridge east of the station led down a long flight of twenty steps to a single platform between the two lines. This platform was some 350 ft long and 30 ft wide; most of its length was covered by a wooden roof. A waiting room, station offices and a small signal box all stood on this single platform. The original station name was Boscombe, which did little to pacify Boscombe's residents, who required a station located properly in their own community. Nor of course did the name satisfy the residents of Pokesdown. As a compromise, in 1891 the station was renamed 'Pokesdown

(Boscombe)'. The suffix remained until 1897 when at last Boscombe acquired its own station.

The years 1930-31 saw the complete rebuilding of Pokesdown Station associated with the quadrupling of the track on this section of the line. The island platform and entrance from the bridge were demolished and two platforms with long canopies were built outside the four tracks. An overbridge connected the two platforms (with two long flights of steps), leading to a new station entrance on Christchurch Road. The station today remains generally in the form of the 1930s re-build.

POOLE

OPENED: 2nd December 1872 (as the terminus of the Broadstone - Poole branch line from the Southampton - Dorchester Railway).
CLOSED: Passengers – remains open for passenger services on the London (Waterloo) - Weymouth line.
Goods – 18th July 1966.

Up until 1872 rail passengers to Poole travelled via the Southampton to Dorchester main line railway, the Poole Junction to Poole branch line and the short toll bridge or ferry crossing to Poole Quay. Poole

Poole. The original station following doubling of the line from Broadstone; a varied set of canopies covers the sharply curved platforms.

Poole. A view east in August 1963 before demolition.

itself received its first station adjacent to the town centre in December 1872 as the southern terminus of the LSWR branch line from Broadstone. This single line was subsequently extended further south east to Bournemouth West on 15th June 1874.

The station was sited on a sharp curve, and gradually developed as business expanded, particularly with the opening of the through line to London via Bournemouth, Brockenhurst and Southampton in 1888. Facilities were also enhanced with the opening of the curved Holes Bay embankment on 1st June 1893, cutting out the circuitous route to Dorchester and Weymouth via Broadstone. From this date Poole Station served two through routes; the Bath to Bournemouth West services of the Somerset and Dorset Railway and the Waterloo to Weymouth services of the London and South Western Railway.

The principal brick buildings, complete with a small bookstall and toilet block, occupied the down platform; these buildings were linked by a wooden canopy of varying heights. The up side facilities included brick built lamp and store rooms and the main bookstall. These buildings survived until 1969, before being demolished for the construction of the new Towngate roadbridge. They were replaced by a featureless clasp type building at the opposite (Wareham) end of the up platform. In 1988 a further new station was constructed largely on the up side, a vaulted roof being suspended from four columns. The down side platform was, at this point, provided with two shelters, the two platforms being linked by a footbridge with no cover. These 1988 buildings largely remain today.

Portesham in the 1930s; a camping coach is sited in the siding (centre).

PORTESHAM

OPENED: 9th November 1885 (with the opening of the Abbotsbury Railway).
CLOSED: Passengers and goods – 1st December 1952 (with closure of the branch line).

Portesham Station, like others on the Abbotsbury branch, was sited on the south side of the single line. A solid building of local stone, its platform was some 233ft long, paved with granite slabs beneath the canopy and otherwise surfaced with loose gravel. The building was a good example of William Clarke's work and, like other stations of his design, access was from the platform and a wooden gate at the side of the building. The general waiting room was divided from the booking office by a wooden partition. The remainder of the building incorporated a ladies' waiting room, a store, lamp room, coal store and toilets. An unusual feature was the roof light in the middle of the canopy which helped illuminate the waiting room.

At the Abbotsbury end a short siding in the 1930s accommodated a GWR camping coach, whose bed linen was brought in every week from the GWR stores at Swindon. Directly opposite the station stood the goods shed (21 x 15ft), much smaller than others on the line.

Like Abbotsbury, Portesham Station was a popular destination for Sunday School trips from the Weymouth area; games and picnics were organised in nearby fields. In August 1962 Portesham station was purchased for residential conversion; it remains in this use today.

OPENED: First station – 16th October 1865 (as terminus of the Weymouth - Portland Railway). Second station – 7th May 1905 (on the Easton and Church Hope Railway).

CLOSED: Passengers – 2nd March 1952 (with the closure of the Weymouth - Portland line to passenger traffic).
Goods – 5th April 1965.

The first station was a basic single terminus platform with a building across the track end. By the turn of the century conditions were cramped for both passengers and goods. In 1896 291,349 tickets were sold at this small station. These large numbers derived partly from building projects under way in the harbour area at that time, with many workers travelling from Weymouth.

The need for improvement was also prompted by the opening of the Easton and Church Hope Railway for passengers on 1st September 1902. This line had been used for goods traffic since 1st October 1900. At the commencement of the new passenger service a temporary wooden platform with a waiting shelter was provided on the new line, linked with the original terminus by a footpath. These arrangements

Portland. Exterior of the first station on 21st April 1904 (See also page 4)

continued for some three years. The original building remained in use as a goods depot until its demolition in February 1969 associated with the construction of the new Victoria Square roundabout.

During 1905 a new through station was completed at a cost of £10,000, the down platform being used from 2nd February 1905 and the up platform from 7th May 1905, this latter date being taken as the formal opening of the new station. The original platforms were constructed in timber but in later years the Southern Railway replaced the 500 ft long platforms with stone and concrete components. A fully enclosed footbridge was provided. On the down platform a general waiting room and gent's toilets were provided while the up platform facilities comprised a waiting room and toilets for both sexes. The buildings were a mixture of brick, corrugated iron and wood; light-weight materials were essential as the station was sited on land reclaimed from Portland Harbour.

The new station was some six feet above the level of the original station in Victoria Square, which had been prone to flooding. Bomb damage occurred during an air raid on 11th August 1940. Following closure of this second station in 1952 it was demolished in April 1954. The site of the original 1865 station is now covered by the Victoria Square roundabout, while the site of the 1905 station is now covered by the ex-Services complex used for many years as a heliport.

POWERSTOCK

OPENED: 12th November 1857 (with the opening of the Bridport Railway from Maiden Newton to Bridport).

CLOSED: Passengers – 5th May 1975 (with closure of the Bridport line).

Goods – 13th March 1961.

Powerstock Station, situated on the up side of the line in the small hamlet of Nettlecombe, was the only intermediate passenger station on the Bridport branch line when it opened. The station building was mainly of stone, a large part being the station master's house. In 1910 the platform was lengthened. Behind the station building there was a small goods yard partly quarried out of the hillside, incorporating two sidings and a small loading platform.

Powerstock. Looking towards Bridport on 27th April 1963; note the large corrugated iron lamp hut.

As from 1936 a six berth camping coach was sited at Powerstock Station, one of about fifty the GWR provided on its system. Powerstock Station became unstaffed as from 11th April 1966; the following year the station building was put on the market and subsequently converted into a house. The platform and track bed now form part of the garden.

RADIPOLE HALT

OPENED: 1st July 1905 (on the Dorchester - Weymouth line, originally opened on 20th January 1857).

CLOSED: 6th February 1984 (official closure date, but no trains had called after 31st December 1983 for safety reasons).

Opened with the introduction of the local steam rail-motor service between Dorchester and Weymouth in 1905, it sought to meet the needs of this expanding suburb of Weymouth. The halt initially comprised two timber built platforms with GWR cast iron pagoda waiting shelters. The old timber platforms were replaced in 1946 by concrete slabs mounted on pre-cast concrete slats but the pagoda huts remained. In August 1974 electric lighting replaced the original gas lights and in June 1977 the old pagoda huts were replaced by 'bus shelters'. All remains of the halt have gone apart from fencing on the original paths leading down to the platforms.

Radipole Halt. Looking south towards Weymouth in the early 1970s; the original GWR pagoda huts remain on the newer concrete platforms.

RODWELL

OPENED: 1st June 1870 (on the Weymouth - Portland Railway, originally opened in 1865). Passenger station only.

CLOSED: 2nd March 1952 (with closure of the Weymouth - Portland line to passenger traffic).

A single platform, 100 ft long, on the east side of the then single line opened in 1870 to serve the nearby developing residential area. The platform housed a small stone built waiting room and booking office;

Rodwell. An early pre-1907 view north towards Wyke Road bridge.

Sandsfoot Castle Halt. Passengers on the last day of services in 1952.

the platform itself was extended in January 1894. A loop line and new up platform came into use on 8th December 1907, thus increasing the Portland line capacity. The main buildings on the down line were also enlarged. The lattice type footbridge also dated from the 1907 additions, as did the GWR pagoda type shelter on the up platform. The main buildings and signal box were destroyed during an air raid on 15th April 1941, the raid killing the only member of staff on duty. The damage resulted in trains calling at Rodwell during daylight hours only until 1945.

Following closure of the station in 1952 the line remained in use for goods traffic until 1965, tracks being lifted in 1970. The original track bed is now in use as a footpath; the remains of the two platforms still exist as does the small entrance gate from Wyke Road and the path to the down platform.

SANDSFOOT CASTLE HALT

OPENED: 1st August 1932 (on the Weymouth - Portland Railway, originally opened in 1865).

CLOSED: 2nd March 1952 (with closure of the Weymouth - Portland line to passenger traffic).

Built at a cost of £340, the halt served both local residents and holiday makers visiting Sandsfoot Castle and Castle Cove. A footbridge was later erected to provide direct access for the residents of the nearby

Sherborne. The William Tite building on the up platform in the late 1920s with book stall and the 1926 arched shelter on the down platform.

Southlands Estate. The simple 300 ft wooden platform on the east side of the single line was faced with old sleepers to contain the solid ash filling. A small wooden shelter provided cover. Some small remnants of the platform structure remain in the undergrowth beside the original line, whose formation is now a footpath.

SHERBORNE

OPENED: 7th May 1860 (as the western terminus of the extension of the Salisbury - Yeovil Railway from Gillingham). Extension to Yeovil opened 1st June 1860.

CLOSED: Passengers – remains open for services on the London (Waterloo) - Exeter line.
Goods – initial closure 5th April 1965, final complete closure 18th April 1966.

The opening was a day of celebration in Sherborne; bells pealed and bands played. A canon was fired and approximately 1200 school children assembled on the slopes overlooking the station. The original plan was for the railway to go north of the town, but the final route passed to the south once the owner of Sherborne Castle withdrew his objections to the railway going near the castle. In return, he stipulated that two fast trains a day should always stop at Sherborne.

Shillingstone. The main buildings on the up platform and the small shelter on the down platform on 7th July 1962.

Throughout its life the two local public schools of Sherborne School (boys) and Sherborne School for Girls have brought extensive patronage. The nearby milk factory also generated considerable goods traffic, as did other commercial activities of the town. The Sir William Tite designed building is constructed in stone from the nearby Ham Hill quarries. The station master's house was incorporated in the buildings on the up platform which also contained the majority of the main station facilities. A covered footbridge was constructed in 1886 though, unusually, this was unglazed. The original shelter on the down platform was replaced by an arched construction in 1926 and this again was replaced by a composite shelter and canopy in 1962. Modern lighting facilities replaced the earlier Southern Railway lighting standards during the 1980s. As with other stations on this line, improvements came in 1993 with the introduction of the Class 159 trains.

The station buildings today remain generally in the form following the 1962 replacement of the down side buildings. The goods shed is in commercial use and part of the goods yard is now a car park.

SHILLINGSTONE

OPENED: 10th September 1863 (with the opening of the Blandford St Mary - Blandford - Templecombe section of the Somerset and Dorset Railway).

CLOSED: Passengers – 7th March 1966 (with closure of the Bath Green Park - Poole line).
Goods – 5th April 1965.

Spetisbury Halt. The original station building and platform on the single line, showing widening in progress.

Sited at the northern end of the mile long village, the station also served nearby Child Okeford and Okeford Fitzpaine. The main station building was on the up platform (towards Sturminster Newton); the most notable feature being the ornate canopy, unusual on stations on the southern section of the Somerset and Dorset Railway. This canopy was supposedly erected in honour of Edward VII who, as Prince of Wales, used the station when shooting at nearby Iwerne Minster House. For some years this up platform had an attractive garden with shrubs and flower beds. The down platform (towards Blandford), though considerably longer, only had a small shelter. Beyond the northern end of the up platform was a goods yard incorporating a loading dock, goods shed, a 5 ton hand crane and a coal yard.

The main station building on the up platform, including the canopy, is still in place, albeit in rather poor condition. The down platform shelter was removed in 1967. Most of the former goods yard is now a car park for a small industrial estate developed on the former station approach road.

SPETISBURY HALT

OPENED: 1st November 1860 (with the opening of the Wimborne - Blandford St Mary section of the Dorset Central Railway).
CLOSED: 17th September 1956.

Adjacent to, and south west of Spetisbury, the station stood a little way above the village. The original booking office and waiting rooms were located on the platform serving the 1860 single line. The line was doubled in 1901 and the new larger scale buildings, built on the new up platform, included a booking office, waiting rooms and a lavatory. Lighting on the platforms was always minimal.

Spetisbury, originally designated as a station, became unstaffed as from 13th August 1934 and was downgraded to a halt as from 1st January 1939. The platforms are still in place and can be reached via steps by the road bridge. No buildings remain, having been demolished in 1958/59.

STALBRIDGE

OPENED: 10th September 1863 (with the opening of the Blandford St Mary - Blandford - Templecombe section of the Somerset and Dorset Railway).

CLOSED: Passengers – 7th March 1966 (with closure of the Bath Green Park - Poole line) .
Goods – 5th April 1965.

Sited less than half a mile north east of the town centre, the station buildings, of typical Dorset Central design, were concentrated mainly on the up platform (town side). Built in brick, they included the station master's house, a booking office and signal box. A shelter provided the

Stalbridge. The main station buildings on the up platform viewed from the south with the level crossing gates in place for rail use.

Stourpaine and Durweston Halt. The concrete platform on the single line on 7th July 1962.

only accommodation on the down platform. There was no footbridge.

A long loop line allowed trains to cross; up trains (towards Templecombe) were, as usual on this line, given the straight run through. A small goods yard, also on the town side, incorporated a goods shed, loading dock, cattle pens and a small hand crane.

Much of the station was demolished in 1967, including the down platform and signal box. The up platform and station house survived until 1972. The sites of the station and goods yard have now been redeveloped (Steel Stockholder ASD Yeovil). The track of a former goods line which was extended during the Second World War to serve a Ministry of Food Depot across the road is still visible across the adjoining road. There is also a slight hump on the road at the site of the former level crossing.

STOURPAINE AND DURWESTON HALT

OPENED: 9th July 1928 (on the Blandford St Mary - Blandford - Templecombe section of the Somerset and Dorset Railway, originally opened in 1863).

CLOSED: 17th September 1956.

Located on a single line section, this halt, a late addition on this line, served Stourpaine village to the north and Durweston to the south west. The simple concrete platform, some 120 ft long, perched precariously on concrete stilts on top of an embankment adjacent to a bridge over a farm track. The platform shelter was provided at a later

Sturminster Newton. Towards Stalbridge in January 1966 showing the up platform buildings and dip leading to the wooden foot crossing.

date; the Southern Railway influence typical of this time is clearly seen in the use of standardised concrete components.

Remnants of the halt remain, with the platform structure still basically in place with some concrete slabs displaced or missing; the shelter has been demolished. The steps to the halt up the embankment on the Stourpaine side still survive, though somewhat overgrown.

STURMINSTER NEWTON

OPENED: 10th September 1863 (with the opening of the Blandford St Mary - Blandford - Templecombe section of the Somerset and Dorset Railway).

CLOSED: Passengers – 7th March 1966 (with closure of the Bath Green Park - Poole line).
Goods – 5th April 1965.

Serving this old market town the station buildings, of Dorset Central Railway design, were of red brick and sited mainly on the up platform. They included a gent's urinal, a ladies' waiting room, gentlemen's waiting room, booking office, store and station master's office. Gas lighting was provided by the adjacent gas works. The up platform always retained its original dip in the edge leading onto a wooden foot crossing, as there was no footbridge. The platforms were slightly staggered, the up platform extending slightly further west (towards Stalbridge) and the down platform extending a little to the east (towards Blandford). A wooden signal box, of LSWR design, stood at the eastern end of the up platform; a water column was at the east end of the down platform.

To the north of the station a large goods yard (with five sidings) provided a number of facilities including a small brick built goods shed. The weekly cattle market to the south of the station generated considerable traffic for many years. The station buildings were demolished in 1973/4 and the entire site has now been redeveloped with roads and a car park covering the former station area, and commercial buildings on the site of the former goods yard and shed.

SWANAGE

OPENED: 20th May 1885 (with the opening of the Wareham - Swanage branch line).
CLOSED: Passengers – 3rd January 1972 (with closure of the Swanage branch line).
Goods – 4th October 1965.
REOPENED: 1975 with the commencement of operations of the preserved Swanage Railway.

The original station building, constructed by Bull & Co of Southampton, incorporated the usual station facilities, a station master's house and a relatively short platform and canopy.

The buildings were extensively rebuilt and extended in 1938 with a longer platform canopy. This rebuilding was carried out in Purbeck stone and blended well with the original station master's house at the Wareham end, which was virtually unaltered. A new window in the gable gave additional light in the booking hall. Many parts of this rebuilding and subsequent additions comprised Southern Railway pre-cast concrete components, including the platforms, fences and lamp standards. Unfortunately the last replaced the original fluted barley sugar type lamp posts. A particular feature of the station was the Benn & Cronin metal indicator outside the station showing train times. The

Swanage.(*Above*) A Wareham bound train in about 1887 in front of the original 1885 buildings including the relatively short canopy. (*Below*) The restored station of the Swanage Railway on 11th June 1999.

station became partially unstaffed as from 8th September 1968.

With the advent of the preserved Swanage Railway major refurbishment has taken place, including the provision of a ticket office and book/gift shop. The buildings also incorporate offices of the Wilts & Dorset Bus Co and a taxi firm. The goods yard now contains a bus station. As well as a car park, part of the site is now occupied by a supermarket. The goods shed has been restored by the Swanage Railway. The station master's house continues to be occupied.

Thornford Bridge Halt. Looking north, the two staggered wooden platforms either side of the road bridge on 7th July 1962.

THORNFORD BRIDGE HALT

OPENED: 23rd March 1936 (on the Yeovil - Weymouth section of the Wilts, Somerset and Weymouth Railway (GWR), originally opened in 1857).

CLOSED: remains open for services on the Bristol - Weymouth line. Trains stop by request only. The suffix Halt was dropped in May 1969 and it became Thornford as from 6th May 1974.

Sited about one mile south west of the village of Thornford, the halt originally comprised two staggered timber built platforms (150ft x 7fift) on the double track line. These were separated by a road bridge which gave access via steps to both platforms (up platform to the north of the bridge, down platform to the south). Both platforms had small wooden shelters lit by oil lamps. The original wooden up platform was replaced by a single concrete platform and shelter transferred from Cattistock Halt when this closed in 1966. With singling of the line the down platform was demolished.

OPENED: 31st March 1862 (on the Bridport Railway, originally opened on 12th November 1857).
CLOSED: Passengers – 5th May 1975 (with closure of the Bridport line).
Goods – 4th April 1960.

Although sited alongside the Bridport Railway, the residents of Toller had to wait nearly five years for their own station. The opening in March 1862 was celebrated with a small festive gathering at Great Toller, at the invitation of Edward Pope, a local squire, who also laid on an excellent lunch for the directors of the railway company arriving on the first train to stop at Toller.

For some thirty years no shelter was provided at the station until, as a result of complaints, the Bridport Railway authorised the provision of a small hut. In 1905 the station was reconstructed; the platform being lengthened at the Maiden Newton end and a new Great Western style wooden building erected. Also provided were a corrugated iron lamp room and a cast iron gent's urinal. At the same time the original goods siding was converted into a loop; a small

Toller. Looking towards Bridport the fine wooden building together with the cast iron gent's urinal, the latter a feature of many early stations..

loading dock was provided which over the years handled a considerable amount of local traffic. Prior to the Second World War, the main goods traffic was milk trains stopping to load and unload churns.

The station became unstaffed on 11th April 1966 and passenger services ceased with the closure of the Bridport line in May 1975. In 1986 the station building was moved to Totnes to form the southern terminus of the South Devon Railway. The platform remains largely intact, although much covered in undergrowth. A public footpath leads towards the platform but much of the trackbed is now in private ownership.

UPWEY

OPENED: 21st June 1871 (on the Dorchester-Weymouth section of the Wilts, Somerset and Weymouth Railway (GWR), originally opened on 20th January 1857). Passenger station only.

CLOSED: 19th April 1886.

Following the opening of the line between Dorchester and Weymouth in 1857, local residents campaigned for a station at Upwey. In 1870 the Great Western Railway agreed, providing the residents contributed £150 towards the cost. Subscription lists were opened and a total of £174 2s was raised; £83 18s 6d by Upwey residents and £90 3s 6d by Broadwey. The station was sited in Broadwey to the north of the railway bridge, spanning what is now known as Old Station Road. Believed to be of timber construction, it was mistakenly spelled 'Upway' for a few weeks. *The Dorset County Chronicle* described it as a 'neat and pretty little station'.

With the opening of the new Upwey Junction Station nearly half-a-mile to the south, this original Upwey Station closed in April 1886; by October 1887 it had been demolished, though it is thought possible that one of its original shelters was transferred to the down platform of the new Upwey Junction Station. No traces of this station remain although its siting is reflected in the road name.

Upwey is the only Dorset station or halt of which no photograph is known to exist.

Upwey (Abbotsbury Branch). Looking towards Abbotsbury from the Dorchester Road bridge.

UPWEY (ABBOTSBURY BRANCH)

OPENED: 9th November 1885 (with the opening of the Abbotsbury Railway).

CLOSED: Passengers – 1st December 1952 (with closure of the Abbotsbury line to passenger and goods traffic beyond Upwey). Goods – 1st January 1962.

Originally opened as 'Broadway' (then Broadwey in June 1891), it was renamed Upwey on 1st January 1913 to avoid confusion with Broadwey in Worcestershire.

The main buildings on the south side of the single line were of local stone with a roof of red and blue tiles alternating every third row, and a canopy. Like others on the branch line, the station was designed by William Clarke and constructed under a sub-contract by Mr Edwin Snook, a local builder from Broadwey.

Before the Second World War a short siding at the west end of the platform was the site of a GWR camping coach. Beyond the station stood a large stone built goods shed, while south of this a long siding served the local coal merchants.

Following the line's closure to passenger traffic in 1952 (when the building was renamed Upwey Goods), some deterioration set in. The station canopy was removed in 1955, having already been shortened.

Upwey Junction. The up platform in the 1930s with the symmetrical canopy covering the up and branch line (left) platforms; also shown the down side shelter.

Goods traffic continued for a further nine years with the track from the main line at Upwey Junction being re-designated as a goods siding as far as the station site.

The whole site was sold by auction on 24th September 1968 and subsequently redeveloped with the original station building being used as offices within a small industrial complex. At the west end of the site a coal merchant uses the original goods shed as offices.

UPWEY JUNCTION

OPENED: 19th April 1886 (on the Dorchester-Weymouth section of the Wilts, Somerset and Weymouth Railway (GWR), originally opened on 20th January 1857). Passenger station only.

CLOSED: remains open for services on the London (Waterloo) - Weymouth and Bristol - Weymouth lines.

This junction station at the point where the Abbotsbury Railway turned west from the main Weymouth to Dorchester line opened in 1886 some five months after the branch line itself. It served both as a transfer point and also as a station for local residents travelling to Weymouth and Dorchester. During the First World War there was also traffic from the nearby Australian Army Camp.

The station was unusual in that the levels of the adjacent up and branch platforms diverged. The up platform served the main line, climbing towards Bincombe Tunnel; whilst the other platform served the Abbotsbury line, beginning its rapid descent. Both platforms were at the same level at the Weymouth end, but the difference at the northern end was very marked, with a massive stone wall separating them. Also unusual was that the branch platform doubled up as the final stage of the approach road to the main station.

The principal timber built buildings were on the up main line platform; these incorporated the station master's office, ticket office, a waiting room and ladies' and gent's toilets. All these opened only onto the up platform. The main entrance to the up platform was up a flight of stairs from the branch platform through the stone wall between the waiting room and the ladies' room. The design of the buildings was symmetrical with the roof extended on either side of the main building, forming narrow canopies. This was just about adequate on the up platform, but practically useless on the branch line as the canopy was so high above the platform.

The down platform was served by a small waiting room, whose style was very different to the buildings on the up platform, and which may have been transferred from the first Upwey Station, just to the north, which closed when Upwey Junction opened. At the end of 1923 this down platform was reconstructed with improved clearance, at a cost of £588. Well kept gardens were a feature of the station.

The branch platform ceased to be used on 1st December 1952 when the Abbotsbury line closed for passengers. The branch track bed adjacent to the station was filled in 1986 using rubble from the old Weymouth station, and a new car park was built. No longer a junction station, its name changed to Upwey and Broadway, and it became unstaffed as from 1st March 1965.

The original buildings were demolished in 1972 and replaced by 'bus shelters'. In April 1987 the up platform was rebuilt at the same time as the Dorchester to Weymouth line was closed for the construction of a new bridge over the Dorchester by-pass. The original lattice girder foot bridge connecting the two platforms was upgraded with new steps being provided. New platform shelters were

Upwey Wishing Well Halt. The wooden platforms before the First World War with a Dorchester bound auto-train; note the pagoda shelter and spelling 'Halte'.

introduced, together with new fencing and lighting. With the arrival of the electric services from Waterloo, Upwey and Broadwey Station was revamped to serve the ever growing suburbs of north Weymouth.

UPWEY WISHING WELL HALT

OPENED: 28th May 1905 (on the Dorchester-Weymouth section of the Wilts, Somerset and Weymouth Railway (GWR), originally opened on 20th January 1857).

CLOSED: 7th January 1957.

The timber built two platform halt with corrugated iron GWR style pagoda huts opened with the commencement of local steam rail-motor services between Dorchester and Weymouth. In 1946 pre-cast concrete huts were erected on the re-built platforms. Lighting was provided by oil lamps.

The halt's main purpose was to serve the 'nearby' tourist attraction of the wishing well in Upwey village – despite the fact that the halt was 1fi miles away uphill. Many visitors did travel to the well by train in the early days, but increasing competition from cars and buses led to the halt's closure. Its distance from Upwey village and the difficult access up steps hindered use by the 'locals'. No traces of the two platforms now remain.

Verwood. Looking north, station staff and a permanent way gang pose for the photographer; the public house can be seen above the station building.

VERWOOD

OPENED: 20th December 1866 (with the opening of the Salisbury and Dorset Junction Railway).

CLOSED: Passengers and goods – 4th May 1964 (with closure of the original Salisbury and Dorset Junction Line).

One of the four original intermediate stations, each with a passing loop on this single track railway, the station primarily served the settlement of Verwood to the east. Two nearby brickworks generated inward coal traffic and outward finished brick products.

The principal station buildings, including a canopy, were sited on the up platform together with a signal box. The down platform was only provided with a shelter. The adjoining goods yard incorporated cattle pens and a crane. Unusually, the Albion Hotel public house stood in the station yard. The whole complex remained basically unaltered for its ninety eight year life, with lighting by oil throughout. The site has now been covered by the realigned B3081 road (realigned that is on the other side of the Albion Hotel), and by new housing development. The original road bridge and a section of the road remains adjacent to the hotel. A short flight of steps that led from the original down platform towards Verwood is still in place leading up from the public house forecourt.

WAREHAM

OPENED: First station – 1st June 1847 (with the opening of the Southampton - Dorchester Railway).
Second station – 4th April 1887 (larger station providing improved interchange facilities with the new Swanage branch railway opened in 1885).

CLOSED: Passengers – remains open for services on the London (Waterloo) - Weymouth line.
Goods – 4th May 1970 (a small siding remained in use for oil products until December 1978).

The first Wareham Station opened with the Southampton to Dorchester Railway on a site east of the present station and the original level crossing. A station master's house stood alongside it. A second station was built west of the level crossing in 1886 (this date can be seen on the down side building) and opened in April 1887. The down bay and up bay platforms sited at the Dorchester end of the station were principally used by the Swanage line trains and overall facilities were much improved. At the east end of the down platform there was originally a pair of crossing keepers' cottages, whilst on the up platform a ticket collectors' shelter and inspectors' office were sited.

Wareham. A rare west view of the first station.

Westham Halt. A small wooden hut by the gate houses the ticket collector in 1951; the platform shelter can be seen above this hut.

The adjacent level crossing to the east of the station became redundant on 3rd April 1980 with the opening of the new road bridge, finally ending the congestion it generated for traffic to and from the coast. The station received a major face lift in 1988 and in the late 1990s more restoration took place.

Wareham Station is a fine preserved example of an LSWR station now over 100 years old (see photograph on page 95). The current station buildings retain many of the original features, including a dormer window which was added to give extra light to the booking office. Good passenger services are provided to Weymouth, Bournemouth and London. In recent years the station has become the starting point and terminus for stopping services to and from the east.

WESTHAM HALT

OPENED: 1st July 1909 (on the Weymouth - Portland Railway, originally opened 1865).

CLOSED: 2nd March 1952 (with closure of the Weymouth - Portland line to passenger traffic).

Opened with the introduction of a local steam rail-motor service on the Weymouth to Portland line, the halt was sited just to the south of the Littlefield level crossing and subway on Abbotsbury Road in Weymouth. The platform on the up (Westham) side of the line was faced with stone and had an iron shelter with a flat roof. At the entrance gate on Abbotsbury Road stood a small wooden hut for the ticket collector who attended at peak times. In July 1946 the platform was rebuilt. The halt was much used by pupils at the nearby Weymouth Grammar School, carrying them from the Isle of Portland and the Rodwell and Wyke areas in the south of the town. The platform remains to the west of the old track bed which is now in use as a footpath to Rodwell and Wyke.

WEST MOORS

OPENED: 1st August 1867 (on the Southampton - Dorchester Railway, originally opened 1847).

CLOSED: Passengers 4th May 1964 (with closure of the Ringwood - Broadstone and Salisbury - Dorset Junction lines to passengers). Goods 20th September 1965 (some army specials until 1974).

This junction station opened some eight months after the Salisbury and Dorset Junction Railway, which veered north from the Southampton and Dorchester Railway just north east of the station site. At its opening the local population was sparse, although this increased markedly in later years; the community of Fern Down (as it

West Moors. A train arrives from Wimborne in August 1958; an unusual concrete component footbridge spans the tracks.

was spelt at the time of the station's opening) was two miles to the south. The signboard stated 'West Moors for Ferndown'. The principal buildings were on the up platform (towards Ringwood); a concrete footbridge was added early in the 1900s. In 1943 the station became the location of a War Department petrol depot.

The site of the station and adjacent goods yard have now been totally cleared and elderly persons' housing erected (Castleman Court). The Castleman Trail passes through the housing site. The railway's past presence is commemorated not only in the name Castleman but also in the adjoining public house 'The Tap and Railway'; this supersedes the previous Railway Hotel.

WEYMOUTH

OPENED: Passengers – 20th January 1857 (as the southern terminus of the Wilts, Somerset and Weymouth Railway (GWR)).
Goods – 2nd March 1857.

CLOSED: Passengers – remains open for services on the London (Waterloo) - Weymouth and Bristol - Weymouth lines.
Goods – 14th August 1972.

Weymouth's growing importance as a resort, following the royal patronage of George III together with its development as a cross Channel port, led to a great demand for rail services. Eventually the Wilts, Somerset and Weymouth Railway (a subsidiary of the GWR) was opened for passengers to the resort in January 1857. At the same time, a new link spur at Dorchester to the Southampton and Dorchester Railway permitted services from London via Southampton, Ringwood and Wimborne. This dual role of Weymouth's new station was complicated by services on the W-S-W Railway being on broad gauge track and the S-D railway services on standard gauge. The track work at the station was thus very complex; the situation was relieved in 1874 when the broad and mixed tracks were abandoned in the area.

The new terminus in King Street, close to the Esplanade, was built on reclaimed marsh and incorporated a sub-structure of trussed timber girders resting on a large number of timber piles. The timber built station with its overall roof and glazed end screens was based on

Weymouth. A general view in 1931; the glazed roof spanning the main central tracks and platforms is flanked by two covered bay platforms.

working drawings of J.H. Bertram, one of Brunel's chief assistants and engineer of the Great Western Railway for eight months after Brunel's death. It was built by a local builder, T. Dodson, for an estimated cost of £10,000. The cost of the whole complex including the station, engine sheds, goods facilities and associated track was some £44,000. At its opening the glazed overall roof spanned two platforms and three centre carriage sidings. In addition on either side of the main roof span, there were shorter covered bay platforms.

Due to the short notice of the opening, celebrations in the town did not take place until 27th January 1857. The day was declared a public holiday, streets were decorated and two triumphal arches decorated in evergreen and bearing the word 'Welcome' surmounted by flags displaying the word 'Freedom' were erected near the statue of George III at the approach to St Mary and St Thomas Streets. The mayor and other dignitaries processed with townsfolk from the Guildhall to the new station, led by the band of the 15th Hussars. Three hundred tickets were donated for residents to ride on an excursion to Yeovil. Festivities continued throughout the day, culminating in a ball at the

Weymouth. The timber buildings on the departure side on 7th August 1981; note the bay window, a feature of some old GWR stations.

Victoria Hotel and a 'sumptuous' dinner at the Royal Hotel at which toasts were made honouring the railway's arrival.

By 1890 the station in its early form was fully developed, and although built and owned by the GWR it was for some years in practice a joint station. Not only were different platforms allocated for the two railway companies, but until 1914 the LSWR appointed its own station master and staff. From that time however the GWR became responsible for running the station.

Increasingly Weymouth grew in popularity with excursions being taken from London, Bristol and Bath. Large numbers of employees from the GWR works in Swindon annually descended on the resort for 'Swindon Week' or later 'Swindon Fortnight'. Local residents recall that for many years both before and after the Second World War the streets of the town were packed with excursionists arriving on trains from all over the country.

With all this increased traffic there were a number of schemes over the years for station redevelopment, one as early as 1909, but more significantly in the late 1930s, when some limited work was undertaken. The glass was removed from the roof in January 1939 as a safety precaution and the overall roof was dismantled in November 1951. Despite its importance and growing congestion, the terminus had remained basically unaltered for nearly one hundred years (1857 - 1951). Partial rebuilding took place in 1956/57 with the construction of two modern full length platforms.

The final major developments came in the 1980s. Demolition of the old station commenced on 13th August 1984 with the new buildings coming into use on 3rd July 1986. The two 1957 platforms were incorporated in the new station and a new platform was built largely for use by Western Region trains. A new sculpture in the station approach/car park area was unveiled on 7th May 1988. The most recent chapter opened on 16th May 1988 when the new Waterloo - Weymouth electrified service began, 131 years after the station opened. The new station, as completed in 1986, remains fully in operation. Apart from the 1957 platforms there are now no remains of the original station, apart from the wall alongside Raneleigh Road.

WEYMOUTH QUAY

OPENED: Passengers – 4th August 1889 (with the opening of the Weymouth Town - Weymouth Quay tramway to passenger traffic).
Goods – 16th October 1865 (with the opening of the tramway to goods traffic).

CLOSED: Passengers – 26th September 1987 (with closure of the Weymouth Quay tramway to scheduled passenger services).
Goods – 1st March 1972.

The original 1889 facility basically comprised a single platform attached to the quay buildings for use by boat trains from London. Major improvements at a cost of £120,000 incorporating two platforms were opened by the Prince of Wales on 13th July 1933. Passenger services ceased between September 1939 and June 1946. A third platform was added in 1961 and in the early 1960s some four to five boat trains used the quay station on summer Saturdays. The early 1970s saw the construction of a new quay building and the third platform came out of use. Falling passenger use led to the withdrawal

Weymouth Quay. The original 1889 passenger station with a boat train.

of passenger services to the quay station in September 1987. The buildings remain in place for passengers using the fast hydrofoil services to the Channel Islands and France.

WIMBORNE

OPENED: 1st June 1847 (with the opening of the Southampton - Ringwood - Wimborne - Dorchester Railway).

CLOSED: Passengers – 4th May 1964 (with closure of the Ringwood - Broadstone line to passenger traffic).
Goods – 28th February 1966 (some 'carted by public' traffic retained until final closure 2nd May 1977).

Wimborne Station could once claim to be the most important station in Dorset. Originally opened in 1847 as a small station on the Southampton to Dorchester Railway, it grew in importance for north-south movements with the full opening of the Somerset and Dorset Railway in 1863. Thus in the 1870s Wimborne served passengers travelling both east-west between London and Weymouth and north-south from Bristol/Bath/Midlands to the south coast at Poole. With the opening of the new coastal route from Southampton to Weymouth via Bournemouth and Poole, and the construction of cut-off routes reducing and, eventually, eliminating north-south movements, Wimborne's paramount position declined rapidly. It closed in 1964, a

Wimborne. Looking south towards Broadstone; note the tall signal box on the up platform

fact that would have seemed incredible a century earlier.

The entire station stood on a curve, adding considerably to the operational difficulties of this once busy junction. Although the station particularly catered for exchange movements there was also some local demand, although the population of Wimborne remained at about 5,000 throughout the life of the station. Facilities changed as the role of the station itself changed. The original down platform was used in the late nineteenth century as an island platform and two bay platforms were added at a later date, although the down bay platform was not used after April 1938. Both platform canopies were extended early in the twentieth century and a separate building developed as a refreshment room. A number of flat roofed extensions of the station buildings were added at various times but no exact dates are recorded. The whole site of the station and goods yard was cleared and mostly levelled by July 1983; an industrial estate covers much of the area. The previous use is only now recorded in the nearby street names 'Station Road' and 'Station Terrace'.

Wool. Towards Wareham on 2nd May 1965 from the footbridge showing the main station buildings (down side), and shelter (up side).

WOOL

OPENED: 1st June 1847 (with the opening of the Southampton - Dorchester Railway).

CLOSED: Passengers – remains open for services on the London (Waterloo) - Weymouth line.
Goods – 1st March 1965.

For many years the station name board recorded the destination of many of those who used it: 'Wool for Lulworth Cove'. Considerable traffic has also been generated through the years by the nearby military establishments at Bovington Camp and the tank and gunnery ranges to the south.

The principal station buildings have always been on the down side. The up side platform with only a shelter is linked to the down platform by an open footbridge. In 1969 the buildings on the down side were replaced by a featureless prefabricated structure. The up side shelter has been replaced by a bus shelter type structure. For some years prior to the Second World War a Pullman camping coach was sited at Wool Station behind the up platform.

The 1969 prefabricated building and 'bus shelter' continue to provide facilities on the two platforms. The name board now states: 'Alight here for Winfrith Technology Centre'.

WYKE REGIS HALT

OPENED: 1st July 1909 (on the Weymouth - Portland Railway, originally opened in 1865).
CLOSED: 2nd March 1952 (with closure of the Weymouth - Portland line to passenger traffic).

Wyke Regis was still rural when the halt opened with the introduction of the local steam rail-motor services to Portland, but its prime purpose was to serve the nearby torpedo works of Messrs Whitehead & Co (later Wellworthys), which had originally opened in the late nineteenth century. The original basic facility on the up (land) side of the single track line was a single wooden platform with a GWR pagoda type shelter. The platform was lengthened in February 1913 and concrete components were introduced; a second flat roofed hut was also provided. These enhanced facilities were required to serve the extra traffic generated during the First World War at the adjacent torpedo factory.

Wyke Regis Halt. Towards Weymouth shortly after its opening in 1909, the only shelter came with the pagoda but this was later supplemented by another small hut.

In September 1946 the halt platform was reconstructed with a stone face. Very limited remains of the concrete sections of the platform can be traced in the undergrowth beside the original track bed, which is now in use as a footpath.

YETMINSTER

OPENED: 20th January 1857 (with the opening of the Yeovil - Weymouth section of the Wilts, Somerset and Weymouth Railway (GWR)).

CLOSED: Passengers – remains open for services on the Bristol - Weymouth line. Trains stop by request only.
Goods – 5th April 1965.

Standing at the eastern edge of the village, the station continues to provide services for the village itself and surrounding area of north Dorset. Much of the traffic through the years has related to short scale work and shopping movements to and from Yeovil. The original stone buildings were in Wilts, Somerset and Weymouth Railway style, with the main facilities on the up platform and a waiting shelter on the down, behind which stood the station master's house.

The goods yard was sited on the up side and north of the station. It served a local coal merchant and a small animal feed warehouse which acted as a distribution point for surrounding farms. An additional siding for a United Dairies depot was added in 1932. The goods yard closed in 1965.

From October 1969 the station became unstaffed; the last station master having been appointed in the late 1950s. Trains now stop in both directions at the old up platform. All the original buildings have been demolished and replaced by a 'bus shelter'. The old station master's house and the adjacent Railway Inn serve as reminders of former days.

Yetminster. Looking north from the adjoining road bridge with the main buildings on the up platform (left); a shelter serves the down platform.

FURTHER READING

Gosling T. and Clement M., *Dorset Railways*, Sutton Publishing, 1999

Gough T. and Mitchell D., *British Railways Past and Present No 29 Dorset*, Past and Present Publishing Ltd, 1996

Hawkins M., *Somerset and Dorset, Then and Now*, David & Charles, 1995

Haysom D. and Parker J., *The Last Days of Steam in Dorset and Bournemouth,* Alan Sutton 1993

Jackson B.L., *The Abbotsbury Branch*, Wild Swan Publications Ltd 1989

Isle of Portland Railways, Vol 2, Oakwood Press 2000

Jackson B.L. and Tattershall M.J, *The Bridport Branch*, Oxford Publishing Co, 1976

The Bridport Railway, Oakwood Press, 1998

Judge C.W. and Potts C.R., *Somerset and Dorset Railway: An Historical Survey of Track Layouts and Illustrations*, Oxford Publishing Co, 1979

Kidner R.W., *Railways of Purbeck (Revised)*, Oakwood Press, 2000

Lucking J.H., *Railways of Dorset*, Railway Correspondence and Travel Society, 1968

Dorset Railways, Dovecote Press, 1982

Maggs C.G., *Branch Lines of Dorset*, Sutton Publishing, 1996

Mitchell V. and Smith K., Middleton Press (various publication dates)

Bournemouth to Evercreech Junction, 1987

Bournemouth to Weymouth, 1988

Branch Line to Lyme Regis, 1987

Branch Line to Swanage, 1986 and (Revised) 1999

Branch Lines around Weymouth, 1989

Branch Lines around Wimborne, 1992

Salisbury to Yeovil, 1992

Southampton to Bournemouth, 1987

Yeovil to Dorchester, 1992

Oppitz L., *Dorset Railways Remembered*, Countryside Books, 1989

Phillips D., *Westbury to Weymouth Line*, Oxford Publishing Co, 1994

Phillips D. and Pryer G., *Salisbury to Exeter Line*, Oxford Publishing Co, 1997

Phillips D., *Salisbury to Exeter - The Branch Lines*, Oxford Publishing Co, 2000

Popplewell L., *Bournemouth Railway History*, Dorset Publishing Co, 1973
Robertson K., *GWR Halts Vol 1*, Irwell Press, 1990
Smith M., *Railways of the Isle of Portland*, Irwell Press, 1997
Stone C., *Rails to Poole Harbour*, Oakwood Press, 1999
Wright A.P.M., *The Swanage Branch - Then and Now*, Ian Allan, 1992

Wareham. A view from the east dated 29th March 1987 of the comparatively unaltered 1885/6 buildings on the down platform.

ACKNOWLEDGEMENTS

The majority of the photographs reproduced in the book are from Lens of Sutton: pages 4, 11, 12, 19, 21, 26, 31, 41, 44, 45, 46, 50, 53 (top),57, 58, 59, 65, 67, 68, 74, 76, 77, 79, 80, 88, 89, 93 and C.L. Caddy of Weymouth: pages 14, 15, 17, 22, 28, 29, 30, 32, 35, 36, 47, 48, 52, 53 (bottom),54, 55, 62, 63 (top),66, 69, 70, 73, 83, 90, 95. The author is very grateful for the permission given for their use. He also thanks the following for their agreement to use illustrations: Dorset County Museum: pages 25, 43, 49, 63 (bottom),72 (top); Wareham Museum: page 81; I.D. Beale: page 34; S. Blencowe: page 24; R. Carpenter (J. Moss Collection): page 40; B. Chennells: back cover; C.G. Maggs: page 86; W. Newman: page 82; G.A. Richardson: frontispiece; and R.C. Riley: page 37. The remaining photographs were taken by the author or are from his collection where the copyright is unknown.

The

DISCOVER DORSET

Series of Books

A series of paperback books providing informative illustrated introductions to Dorset's history, culture and way of life. The following titles have so far been published.

BRIDGES *David McFetrich and Jo Parsons*
CASTLES AND FORTS *Colin Pomeroy*
CRANBORNE CHASE *Desmond Hawkins*
CUSTOMS *Peter Robson*
DRESS AND TEXTILES *Rachel Worth*
FARMHOUSES AND COTTAGES *Michael Billett*
FARMING *J.H.Bettey* FOLLIES *Jonathan Holt*
FOSSILS *Richard Edmonds* GEOLOGY *Paul Ensom*
THE GEORGIANS *Jo Draper*
THE INDUSTRIAL PAST *Peter Stanier*
ISLE OF PURBECK *Paul Hyland*
LEGENDS *Jeremy Harte* MILLS *Peter Stanier*
PORTLAND *Stuart Morris* POTTERY *Penny Copland-Griffiths*
THE PREHISTORIC AGE *Bill Putnam*
RAILWAY STATIONS *Mike Oakley*
REGENCY, RIOT AND REFORM *Jo Draper*
THE ROMANS *Bill Putnam*
SAXONS AND VIKINGS *David Hinton*
SHIPWRECKS *Maureen Attwooll*
STONE QUARRYING *Jo Thomas*
THE VICTORIANS *Jude James*

All the books about Dorset published by The Dovecote Press are available in bookshops throughout the county, or in case of difficulty direct from the publishers.
The Dovecote Press Ltd, Stanbridge,
Wimborne, Dorset BH21 4JD
Tel: 01258 840549 www.dovecotepress.com